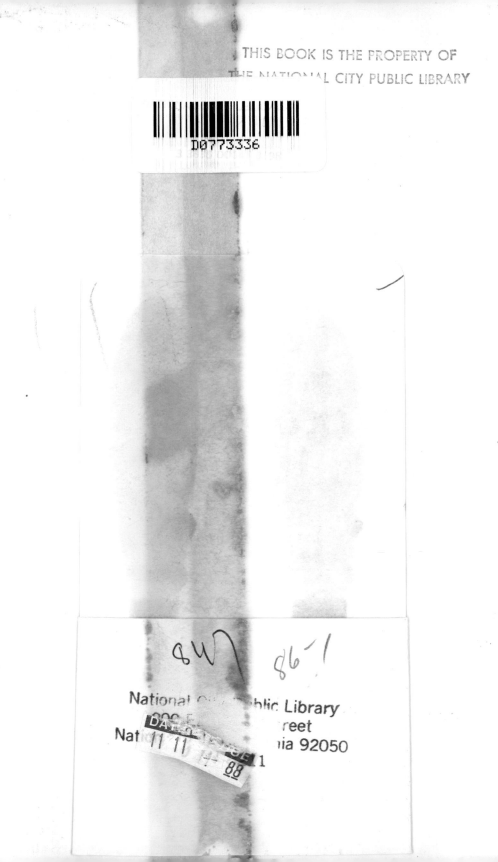

HOME GUIDE TO EARLY READING

HOME GUIDE TO EARLY READING

with reading readiness games and exercises for your preschool child

by Toni S. Gould
illustrated by Jo Farenkopf

Walker and Company

New York

First published in the United States of America in 1976 by the Walker Publishing Company, Inc.

Published simultaneously in Canada by Fitzhenry & Whiteside, Limited, Toronto.

ISBN: 0-8027-0531-6

Library of Congress Catalog Card Number: 75-40825

Printed in the United States of America.

10 9 8 7 6 5 4 3 2 1

to Kathy with love

CONTENTS

PREFACE

Today, more and more emphasis is being placed on the child's experiences with learning in his early years. These experiences are crucial in aiding or hindering his later growth in learning. One of his first learning experiences is reading. Success in learning to read gives the child a feeling of competence in one of his first intellectual endeavors, and develops in him an ever-increasing confidence in his ability to learn and think. Difficulty in acquiring this skill can have crippling effects on the child's ability and willingness to learn in the future.

Basic to this book is the idea that children enjoy learning to read when the experience is a challenge to their minds, when they understand, not memorize, every step in the learning process. In this way, the child's cognitive growth is significantly stimulated in the very process of learning to read.

Before children can actually learn to read, they have to develop certain skills. In the 1940s and 1950s the notion prevailed that such reading readiness would develop spontaneously around six or six-and-a-half years of age, and until that time a child should be shielded from a formal exposure to letters and numbers. In the sixties and especially in the seventies we have come to know that reading readiness must be nurtured in the young child by proper environmental stimulation: that readiness, in effect, can and must be taught.

Teachers in early childhood education, particularly those involved with day care centers and Head Start programs, have consulted me on how to teach readiness most effectively, so that children will meet with success in learning to read. In every instance, we have been able to put into action a structured readiness program which developed every single readiness skill including sound-letter knowledge. There was no pressure to reach definite goals. The children's actual achievement varied from mastering six letters successfully to reading fluently by the end of the year. It is immaterial how much they mastered; what matters is that they acquired a thorough grasp of what they had learned so far.

The specific approach that I have used in teaching children to read, both privately and as a consultant in inner city school classes, is called Structural Reading. This approach, while not the only way to teach reading, has been a most effective way of teaching reading *through insight*. It includes a complete readiness program, which because of its structured sequence has proven suitable for all children. Its success to a large extent has been due to the fact that the teaching materials are self-teaching; hence a child is able to make independent discoveries and correct his own errors.

How does Structural Reading differ from other teaching methods? In contrast to the sight or phonetic approaches, its emphasis is on understanding the actual structure of the spoken, later of the written, word. This approach does not depend on memorization but on teaching the correspondence between sounds and letters according to a carefully graded systematic sequence which enables the child to figure out words on his own from the start. Spontaneous comments, taken down verbatim in a classroom or in a private one-to-one teaching situation, show that children enjoy learning to read when the learning process makes sense to them and allows for independent discovery.

Every parent or teacher must understand the total learning-to-read process if he is to become knowledgeable as to which specific games or activities develop reading readiness and which do not. This book gives the adult the general understanding of the dynamics of the learning process that underlies learning to read. There are many books available which encourage parents to teach their children to read, but there are very few if any that explain how to develop reading readiness systematically, so a child will be prepared to experience continuing success.

This book also presents the step-by-step teaching sequence that leads a child from general readiness activities to learning specific sound-letter correspondences and eventually his first words and sentences. A list of games and activities is included for use with individual children in a one-to-one teaching situation or with small groups of children.

While I am addressing this book primarily to parents who, under our present educational system, are the single most important persons responsible for a child's early learning environment, I also want to reach teachers in early childhood education. Many teachers in this area have put pressure on me to write down my suggestions and experiences as I present them in workshops. I hope to be of help in their all-important venture of developing reading readiness in young children.

This book is not written for the success-oriented parent who wants to produce a super-child who will blitz his peers. It is intended for those who want to recognize and encourage their child's potential in all areas, for those who want to challenge his mind without pressuring him to perform. It is not at all important how much or how fast a child actually learns, for the emphasis in this book is not on achievement, but on the learning process itself.

It is important, however, for parents to understand how to nurture readiness skills essential for learning to read and how to provide materials that will allow a child to learn by insight rather than rote. Specific suggestions are given on how to develop reading readiness. Chapters five through seven describe many readiness activities and games which children enjoy and which can be made. Chapter eight presents detailed suggestions for home-made materials and games which enable children to discover the correspondence of sounds and letters. Chapter nine outlines how to set the stage for reading.

Just as there are natural musicians, there are children who seem to be natural readers; they push their relatives relentlessly to teach them to read. Obviously, these children would learn to read regardless of method or approach, but *how* they are taught in the beginning will have a great influence on their development and their ability to think things through for themselves.

Other children do not push to learn to read at an early age. They may have been late talkers, slow in handling a pencil or brush, unable or uninterested in remembering the names of colors, or, in learning to write their names, show a tendency to form certain letters backward. These children should be helped early. Allowed to develop reading readiness skills at their own pace, they will experience success in an area where they might otherwise meet with failure.

In twenty years of teaching four- and five-year-olds to read, I have found that the child with learning disabilities needs a great deal more careful help than the average child in preparing him for learning to read. At the preschool level he has the interest and, not insignificantly, the free time for it.

Chapter eleven presents case studies of children with serious learning problems who were referred to me before they went to kindergarten. In contrast to remedial work with failing children whose apprehension and anxiety about failure often compounds the original learning disabilities, Bobby and Lisa learned to read, experiencing success at every step in the learning process. The comments of numerous other young children with learning disabilities also included in the book show their growing confidence in their learning ability. They demonstrate how an early start can prevent later failure.

We know, of course, that many children are fortunate and possess no learning disabilities. They learn to read by, or in spite of, any method. But how the child learns, the degree to which the experience draws on and expands his understanding and intelligence, can have a lasting effect on his future intellectual development.

ACKNOWLEDGMENTS

Until this book, my mother, Catherine Stern, and I collaborated on every project. I learned from her not only how to teach children reading but also that children enjoy learning and grow in mental stature when challenged intellectually. I am grateful to her for allowing me to modify the Structural Reading Program into a book for parents. My mother died before this book went to press, but she read the original manuscript and penciled in some corrections.

My friend, sister-in-law, and previous coauthor, Margaret B. Stern, also encouraged me to adapt our Structural Reading approach in this fashion, an encouragement for which I am very grateful.

I am grateful to Random House for allowing me to adapt the teaching approaches and some of the games of the Structural Reading approach to this book. Much of the material in chapters seven and eight is covered at great length in the teachers' guides to the Readiness Books and the first decoding book (Book B: *We Discover Reading*) of the Structural Reading Program.

Several parents helped me on the original manuscript with their comments and suggestions. While space does not permit me to mention by name everyone who helped me, I want to single out Joan Luikart, who worked through portions of the original manuscript and helped me with her thoughtful comments, and Gladys Moon, who gave me valuable suggestions, both as a mother and as an editor.

Deep-felt gratitude goes to Jean Read, whose master touch is visible on every page of the present manuscript. Her instant grasp of what I wanted to say, her insistence that I say it as succinctly as possible, her rare gift for cutting unnecessary detail, all improved the book immensely. Working with her has been an intellectual pleasure as well as a challenge.

The book also owes much to my teachers, colleagues, and friends from whose contact and discussions I benefited, and most particularly to Gene Shalit and Irving Goodman, who suggested that the book be written and who convinced me that parents needed to know how to develop reading readiness and how reading should be taught. Mr. Shalit has been interested in the Structural Reading text from the beginning, and he showed his faith and his support of the program at all times.

More recently, Professor Mariann Winick, head of the Early Childhood Department at Lehman College, encouraged me with specific and valuable suggestions. Felix R. Bremy, time and again, was willing to discuss difficult points with me, and his penetrating logic helped me to clarify my own thinking. Richard Winslow, my editor at Walker, was tremendously helpful in making this book more effective as a practical guide for parents. Finally, I am indebted to Abigail Woods, Louise Callahan, and Gladys Moon for contributing valuable suggestions, as mothers and as experts in the field, to the compilation of children's books.

To protect my pupils I have changed their names and sufficiently altered each family situation so that they cannot be identified. However, the essential parts of the records and all of the children's comments are reproduced verbatim. It was a challenge and a joy to observe these children, and I often learned as much as I taught. Their parents, through their cooperation and support, did much to make the job easier and more productive.

I am grateful to my sons Tim and Jeff for helping me with difficult issues and for suggesting solutions. I want to thank my daughter Kathy for her encouragement, her willingness to discuss learning and teaching problems, and her subtle yet steady insistence that I not give up working on the book.

I rewrote part of the book in the quiet and peace of Garnet Hill on 13th Lake in the Adirondacks, a place of such unspoiled beauty that it is conducive to writing.

Toni S. Gould
Instructor in Early Childhood
Herbert H. Lehman College, CUNY
December 16, 1975

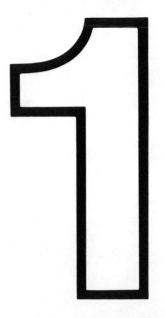

LEARNING
THROUGH INSIGHT

Bruce, age four, who had just completed some informal reading readiness tests, lingered at the door of the study. When asked what he wanted, he said, "I don't want to go. I came to learn to read today."

While his optimism goes beyond the realm of possibility, Bruce is a perfect example of the very strong motivation that most young children have for learning to read. All children start out with a healthy, boundless curiosity to investigate the world about them, and this curiosity includes wanting to know what those strange squiggles on signs and in books say.

At the turn of the century Maria Montessori, while working with retarded children from the slums of Rome, came to the conclusion that young children enjoy learning to read, write, and do arithmetic in the same way that they enjoy games. We grown-ups make an arbitrary distinction between learning and playing. Children do not.

From the time that young children watch older siblings and adults around them pick up books and become absorbed, they want to learn to read. To them this is a skill which provides the entrance ticket to the grown-up world. Because of their spontaneous interest, learning to read, while not accomplished in one day, can become the most challenging and thrilling adventure in their lives.

There is general agreement that reading is *the* single most important skill a child can possess. It is the one that is taught earliest and continued longest. What is often overlooked is the fact that teaching children to read is fascinating for the teacher as well and not that difficult. The crux of the problem is to find ways of teaching which will capitalize on the child's natural interest.

Unfortunately, reading experts do not agree on what kind of reading approach is best suited to capture the child's interest. At this point a presentation of their opposing viewpoints would only leave you confused since you have no basis for deciding which theory is sound. To give you such a basis let's have a look at the teaching of reading from a broader frame of reference, namely that of the psychology of learning and teaching. After we have established some criteria for what constitutes the best learning conditions, we can apply these to the specific problem of learning to read. What kind of learning captures a child's interest and motivates him to pursue an activity?

Psychologists agree that basically there are two kinds of learning: learning through understanding and learning through memorizing. Learning through understanding is a challenge to a child's intelligence; learning through memorizing is merely a demand on his memory. Children are excited when they are able to figure out a problem on their own. In fact, a child's first mental efforts at grasping an idea marks the advance from the toddler who experiments predominantly on a physical basis and the somewhat older child who has realized he can think.

Max Wertheimer, who founded the School of Gestalt Psychology in Berlin in 1913, developed the theory that learning by insight is not only more productive than learning by memorizing but also more enjoyable for the pupil as well as for the teacher. "Every good teacher enjoys teaching and learning when really sensible learning takes place: when eyes are opened, when real grasping, real understanding occurs, when the transition takes place from blindness or ineptness to orientation, understanding, mastery, and when, in the course of such happenings, mind develops."[1]

Most parents will be able to recall incidents from everyday life which illustrate their child's excitement when he first grasped a new idea. The stories which follow happened in nonteaching situations.

Peter, age four, perched on a stool, playing at the kitchen sink. He poured water into an empty milk bottle. Then he stuck a cork into the bottle. When he wanted to retrieve the cork it would not come out. He turned the bottle upside down: the water poured out but not the cork. He stood there. angry and confused. Almost absentmindedly he turned the bottle right side up and turned on the water. The bottle filled and overflowed. Out came the cork. Peter's face lit up. "Oh!" he exclaimed excitedly.

[1] Wertheimer, Max, Foreword to G. Katona, *Organizing and Memorizing* (New York: Columbia University Press, 1940).

For the next half hour Peter repeated the experiment. No one could entice him away from the sink.

While Peter's solution to the problem was accidental, he was thrilled with his achievement. The excitement generated by his discovery motivated him to repeat the experiment over and over again. He was learning through insight.

Children do not enjoy memorizing ready-made answers. They prefer the kind of learning situation where they are the active participants. Understanding how something works produces a feeling of achievement in the child.

Beth, age three, sat down in front of a counting board which had different-sized blocks and slots to match. Taking out the blocks was easy for her, but putting each block back into its proper groove was difficult. "This doesn't go," she said to herself. "Too big." She kept trying to fit the block into two more places until she found the proper groove for the block. She had relatively little difficulty with the smaller blocks, but it took a lot of experimenting to find the right place for the longer blocks. Once she stamped her foot, muttering, "It sticks out." Eventually each block was in its place. Beth beamed. Immediately, she took out all the blocks and started the game over again.

Beth understood the task; hence, she was able to correct her errors. When she played the game again, she could find the proper groove for each block more quickly. Her sense of achievement was written all over her face.

In recent years learning psychologists have stressed the importance of learning through understanding. Drawing conclusions from their own extensive and impressive research they have pointed out that the quality of early learning experiences affects a child's cognitive development. And their findings show that learning through understanding is far more effective than learning through memorizing. Jerome Bruner, formerly head of the Center for Cognitive Studies at Harvard University, clearly states that all children learn better if they "understand structure . . . in short, learn how things are related."[2]

Admittedly, some subject matter cannot be understood because it has no structure. By its very nature it can only be learned through memorization. Whenever we are dealing with names of things or with isolated facts—facts which exist without inherent logic—we cannot learn them through understanding. The capital of Florida, how many people live in New York City, or the exact year in which the United Nations was founded are facts which can only be learned through memorizing.

In other areas of knowledge facts are related. They are part of a logical design which can be understood. School subjects such as arithmetic and geometry have structure, and children learn these subjects better if they are led to understand this structure. Grasping a general principle means an economy in learning; there is *less* to learn.

Learning by insight is a far more productive way of learning than mere memorizing, for it produces transfer. Transfer means that children are able to apply their learning to related tasks. Instead of having to rely on the teacher to provide every answer, children are able to figure out answers on their own.

Learning by insight also has a positive effect on the child's ability to remember. While children should not learn through blind memorization, they must, of course, be able to remember what they have learned. Remembering is easier when children have understood the underlying structure and can thus reconstruct a given fact. Jerome Bruner stresses this point in beautifully concise terms. "An unconnected set of facts has a pitiable short half-life in memory. Organizing facts in terms of principles and ideas from which they may be inferred is the only known way of reducing the quick rate of loss of human memory."[3]

To make mistakes is natural in any learning situation. However, errors that happen in learning through blind memorization are the occasion for a decrease in learning effi-

[2] Bruner, Jerome S., *The Process of Education* (New York: Vintage Books, 1963), p.7.

[3] Bruner, page 31.

ciency and in motivation. When a teacher says "wrong!" the child not only feels diminished, but he will often acquire lasting feelings of uncertainty. When he comes up against this same fact he feels helpless, in effect saying to himself, "I can't remember which answer was wrong and which was right."

On the other hand, when children learn by insight, errors assume a useful function: children are able to learn from their errors. The errors become the occasion for more learning, and this gives the child increased confidence that he has now mastered this particular area of difficulty. An example from the teaching of arithmetic will clarify this last point.

Lisa, age 8, came in for her weekly lesson, very upset. "I'll never get the zero facts, never." She handed me the test she had taken at school on which she had done very poorly. The first row looked like this:

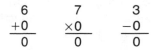

"I just can't remember when the answer is zero," she added in tears. I put aside the test and gave Lisa a block that was four units long. The following dialogue took place:

I: "Add nothing to the 4-block. What do you have now?"

Lisa: "I still have the 4-block."

I: "Take nothing away from the 4-block. What do you have now?"

Lisa: "I have the 4-block."

I: "Let's write down what we just did." Together we recorded the two arithmetic examples. Lisa filled in the answers completely on her own.

$$4 + 0 = 4$$
$$4 - 0 = 4$$

I: "Now give me zero times the 4-block."

Lisa: "You don't get anything if I give it to you zero

times. That's not giving it." Together we recorded that
fact as

4 × 0 = 0

We repeated the experiment once more with a different
block, and then Lisa made up some examples on her own
while I copied over the test she had taken in school. At
the end of the lesson I gave Lisa the test. She solved every
one of the examples correctly. "I got it," she beamed.
"They can't trick me again."

To summarize: We have seen that learning through understanding produces the best learning conditions. It results in transfer and discovery, in an easy and reliable way
of reconstructing facts, and it gives errors their sensible
function of increasing rather than decreasing understanding. Such success in learning directly affects the learner's
motivation; it heightens the interest that already exists.

It follows that in the specific area of learning to read a
child should also learn through understanding, not
through rote memorization. The crucial question is *how*
did he learn to read? Was every step in the learning process intelligible? Was he able to participate actively in the
learning process? Was he able to make discoveries on his
own, independent of the teacher? In the process of learning to read did he use and stretch his mind or merely train
his memory?

Having established some criteria for how children learn
most productively, let us apply them to some different approaches to the teaching of reading. There are four major
approaches to the teaching of reading. Historically, and
speaking of this century only, the phonics approach came
first.

In the old-fashioned phonics approach, a teacher would
write a letter such as m on the board, and inform the class
that this letter says [m].

Key for Reader

[m]
Throughout this book a letter inside brackets will refer to
its sound when it starts a word. For instance, it can refer

to the initial sound of the spoken word [man], a short "mmm" sound without any vowel following.

m
All italicized letters will refer to the printed form of the letter. You will be shown in chapter eight how to teach your child to respond to the printed letter *m* by its sound [m].

ă, ĭ
When you see this mark above a vowel, it means you give its sound name, the sound you hear in the word ăpple, or the word ĭnk.

ā, ī
When you see this mark above a vowel, it means you give its long vowel name, as in words like cāne and pīne.

The children would obediently chorus the [m], attempting to glue a meaningless name to a meaningless visual configuration. After the class had memorized the sound names of all the letters of the alphabet, they were taught to put the sounds together to form words.

This next step was usually drilled in a two-step blending process:

m + a = [mă]
ma + n = [măn]

Unfortunately, this blending process was so difficult that children often called the sounds "[m] [a] [n]" without comprehension. Although they arrived at the pronunciation of the single sounds, they failed to achieve the next important step of connecting the sounds with the spoken word. Thus they did not complete the reading act, for they did not succeed in putting the printed word into the context of the living spoken language. Reading without comprehension is not reading.

There is no doubt that knowing the sound names of the alphabet gave the child the useful tool of being able to sound out words. However, the learning process by which he acquired this tool was unproductive; he had to memorize twenty-four separate letters as isolated configurations without reference to the meaningful spoken language. The learning process did not provide him with sensible clues that would enable him to figure out what a letter said by using his intelligence. He could only master the names of the letters of the alphabet if he had a good memory. Nor did the next phase, learning to blend sounds, allow for learning by insight. Adding up letters in piecemeal fashion did not give the child insight into the structure of the written word. Because the drill on separate sounds was mechanical, the child very often did not even grasp the fact that the written word stands for a spoken word, that reading in essence is listening to the written instead of the spoken word.

Because learning through memorizing is difficult and the rate of forgetting is high, as we know from the previous discussion on learning, a great deal of repetitious drill was necessary to fix the letter knowledge and blending in a child's memory. In most classrooms the phonics instruction was administered very much like bad-tasting medicine. There were many children who learned in spite of the tedious drill, but they did not experience the enjoyment associated with learning to read.

Around 1930, William S. Gray, the American reading specialist, and his followers, determined to rescue children from this old-fashioned phonics drill, designed the sight method as a sensible approach that would center on comprehension as the focal point of reading instruction. They based their theory of reading on the following observations.

The mature reader does *not* pay attention to individual letters; instead he looks at whole words, attaining the meaning instantly. It seems sensible, then, to use the mature reader's performance as a guide for teaching the beginner. Reading instruction should start with sight reading of whole printed words, so that from the very first moment, the beginning reader experiences that reading consists of acquiring *meaning* from the printed word. This will make the reading come alive and motivate the child to want to learn to read more, since he is no longer subjected to meaningless drill. This argument sounds seductively plausible until we investigate *how* in actual practice children are taught to read by this method.

In the sight method, which is also called the look-say approach, the teacher writes a word like *city* on the board and pronounces it; the children are to *look* at it and then *say* it. They then take turns repeating what the word says.

The same teaching approach is followed when reading from a preprimer or a primer. The teacher tells the children what each word says, and they memorize what they are told. Although the child knows the spoken word, as the teacher pronounces it, he has no means of unlocking the printed word for himself, for he has not learned the sounds of the letters.

In this beginning stage single words are taught as if they have no relation to each other, as if they were *names* of visual configurations. Since memorizing names is difficult and the rate of forgetting is high, this beginning vocabulary must be repeated over and over again.

Advocates of the sight approach realize the difficulty of memorizing the visual configurations of a great number of words and therefore advocate helping the child's memory by providing additional clues. The teacher draws the children's attention to the particular configuration of each word as one aid to memory. She encourages children to guess at a word using the accompanying picture or the context of the sentence or the story as a clue.

After about fifty sight words have been introduced, the teacher gives children phonic clues. But this phonics instruction is not a systematic teaching of all the letters; instead, phonics is taught as back-up to the sight reading process. If, for instance, the word *mother* appears in the primer, the teacher explains in the ensuing lesson that the *th* stands for the sound [th]. Since the phonic clues are handed out in piecemeal fashion—a lesson on initial consonants here, a lesson on final consonants there, then several lessons on vowels or word families—they are helpful only in a sporadic fashion. Haphazard instruction of phonics does not provide the beginner with a secure and systematic foundation for accurate reading.

On the surface the sight method looks not only impressive but also attractive, for it surrounds children with a word-filled environment. They start out learning with a real book in front of them or by reading an experience chart. The magic of this "instant reading" is replaced by grim reality when the children themselves realize that they do not have a reliable tool to unlock old and new words accurately. Ultimately they are penalized for the easy beginning, because learning to read by sight has serious and far-reaching disadvantages.

Guessing at a word in a primer or an experience chart does not interfere with comprehension. Children can get the gist of the relatively simple story without knowing what each single word says exactly. Yet guessing is a disastrous habit to acquire, because eventually it has to be unlearned. Guessing at a word may hinder the child from being able to comprehend the exact meaning the author intended. By third grade, at the latest, work in all subjects requires precise reading. Misreading just one word has often prevented a child from being able to solve an arthmetic problem or follow directions in a social studies text.

Since children who learn to read by the sight method do not achieve a consistent understanding of the structure of words, they are not able to transfer their reading knowledge to related words. Knowing the word "Stop" does not automatically enable them to read the word "top" or "Bus Stop." Memorizing one visual configuration is a help only in being able to read that particular word; experience shows that it does not give the clue to figuring out related words.

Since children taught by the sight technique cannot figure out new words on their own most of the time, they must ask what each new word says. Or, if they have misread a word, they depend on the teacher to correct their errors. But this very dependence eliminates the possibility of independent discovery and impedes their intellectual development. Furthermore, they miss out on the sense of achievement that results from learning by insight.

The sight method changed the surface appearance of learning to read, but it did not change the basic learning process which is rote memorization. Instead of memorizing letters and sounds, they memorized words.

Children themselves have an acute awareness of how they are learning to read. Their comments reveal, to an astonishing degree, the fact that *they* know the difference between memorizing and reading.

Nancy, a first grader of two months' standing, came home early one afternoon.

"Nancy," her mother called from the living room, "I have time for you right now. Bring your book and read it to me."

"Mom," replied Nancy materializing at the doorway with a big grin, "I left my book at school, but I can read it to you anyway.

Go, go, go	Help Jane.
Go, Dick, Go.	Go help Jane.
Help, help!	Go, Jane.
Look, Dick.	Go, Jane, go.
Dick! Dick!	Look, Dick."

A seven-year-old pupil whom I had been tutoring wanted to borrow one of my books, but warned me: "I can't take *Green Eggs* and *Ham*, because I memorized that when I was little."

Nicky (6:7),[4] who had been taught to read by the Structural Reading method at home, commented on his first two months of traditional first grade. "I don't get it. Granny taught me to read, but at school Mrs. X teaches us to pretend to read."

Many children do learn to read by the sight method, provided they have good visual memories. However, it has proven disastrous for children with poor visual memories. Recent research studies[5] have confirmed that it is the good

---

[4] Throughout this book, numerals in parentheses after a child's name denote his age. The numeral before the colon refers to the year; the one after the colon denotes the months. The months are noted because significant changes can occur in less than a year with preschool children.

[5] de Hirsch, Katrina, Jansky, Jeannette J., and Langford, William S. in their book *Predicting Reading Failure*, (New York: Harper & Row, 1966), have come up with the fascinating results that intelligence, as measured by an IQ score "ranked only twelfth among predictive measures" of subsequent success in learning to read; eleven other kindergarten tests, the majority of which appraised some aspect of visual memory, were better predictors.

visual memory that counts in learning to read, and children without this, no matter how bright, may be doomed to failure. Their intelligence is no guarantee that they will be able to learn to read.

However, whether or not intelligence is made use of in learning to read is determined to a great extent by the "how" of teaching. A method of teaching reading that is based on rote memorization forces a child to learn by rote; he has no other options. Not all of us are endowed with the gift of visual memory; yet in the sight method visual memory is all-important, and the bright child, like others, is forced to rely on it. He is given no opportunity to use his reasoning.

Paradoxically, the child who is the most intellectually capable often fails to learn to read because he is not taught so that he can use his intelligence to learn. This unnecessary failure invariably results in emotional damage and further learning problems.

The sight method may have brought changes to the appearance of the learning situation. But the real solution is to change the dynamics of the learning process from within, so the beginning reader can learn to read through understanding.

To understand what needs to be done, let's look at the task of the beginning reader. Learning to read is dynamically different from the reading you do as an experienced reader. Your eyes sweep over a page taking in whole words at a time, comprehending words, sentences, and even paragraphs in a flash. You, the accomplished reader, no longer need to pay attention to the individual letters that make up a word.

But we cannot take the accomplished skill of the expert as a teaching model for the beginner. Your expert skill is the end product of a learning process, one that the beginner has to learn from the beginning.

It is usually difficult for a grown-up to empathize with just what learning to read means to a child. You recognize a familiar word instantly, without remembering how once, long ago, you had to decipher it. Perhaps a good way to dramatize the difference between two diametrically opposed approaches to reading is to present words to you with symbols you don't know.

Look at these two "words" for two minutes and then cover them.

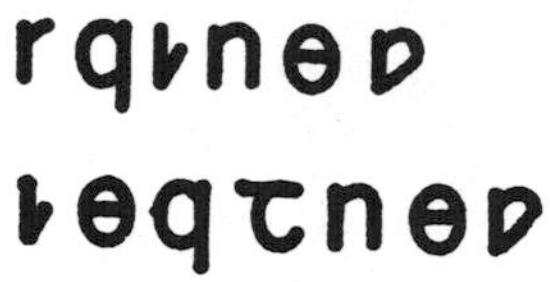

rqɩneᴅ

ⱶeqᴄneᴅ

Figure 1.1.
Two sample words with made-up symbols

Now pick out the two words from the list of eight words below.

ɯeqɩneᴅ

ⱶeqᴄneᴅ

rɪguᴅe

peᴅnqps

ⴉoⱶneᴅ

ⱶᴅqɪn

rqɩneᴅ

ᴅeqⱥɪng

Figure 1.2.
Eight "words" with made-up symbols

Now, how did you determine which configurations in the list were the same as the first two? Could you in any way reason it out? More likely, you relied on visual memory which, by the way, is far better developed in and far more experienced by the adult than the young child. But now, suppose I make it much simpler for you by giving you a code that will enable you to figure out each word? (See figure 1.3.)

You can easily *read* the words once you have the simple code. Even if I changed all twenty-four letters of the alphabet into symbols, you could intelligently figure out any number of words under the same code. You can, of course, check back to the code while you are learning it, but you are not forced to depend on remembering each group of configurations as a whole. Compared to the beginning reader you also have a headstart, because some of my code letters look familiar to you, and, of course, you do actually know how to read English. The child has to progress more slowly, but he, too, needs to have a code, so that he can figure the letters out intelligently rather than rely on an accurate visual memory of them.

It is easier and far more productive to learn the twenty-four symbols of our alphabet than to memorize fifty unrelated sight words. The code of the alphabet unlocks accurately all of the regular words in the English language and, in no small measure, helps with the reading of irregular words.

The first major task of beginning reading instruction is to teach this code without turning the clock back to the outmoded phonics drill. We must find a way of teaching the code that allows for learning by insight, so that the pupil can participate actively in the learning process from the very beginning, using his intelligence and not his memory.

The second major task is to control the reading vocabulary presented to the beginning reader, so that it reveals the structure of the written language. This brings us to the third major approach to the teaching of reading, namely the linguistic one. In 1942, Leonard Bloomfield, the American linguist who pioneered in the field of reading, challenged the sight method's rationale that the first reading vocabulary must present words that are in the child's speaking vocabulary. Bloomfield maintained that if the beginning vocabulary contains irregular words like *look*,

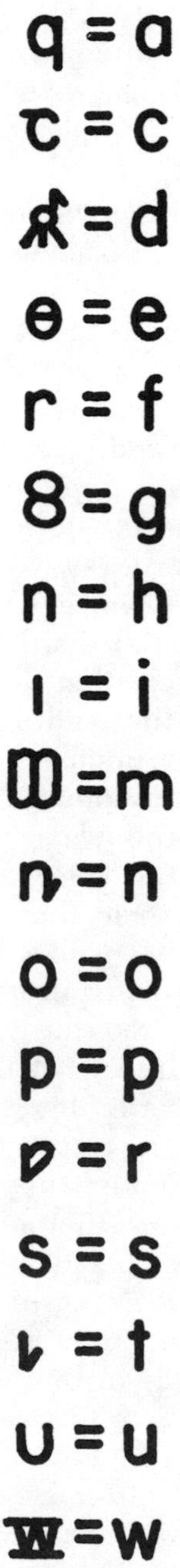

q = a

ᴛ = c

ℛ = d

θ = e

r = f

8 = g

n = h

ı = i

ɯ = m

ɲ = n

o = o

p = p

ᴅ = r

s = s

ʋ = t

u = u

ᴡ = w

Figure 1.3.
The symbols on the left represent the letter on the right.

come, go, and *to,* frequently found in primers using the sight approach, the child will be confused. He has just met words with four different sound values for *o.* The next time he sees a word with an *o* in it, which sound value for the *o* should he use?

Those experts who follow the linguistic approach believe that to be able to use the code successfully, i.e. learn to decode, the beginning reader must at first be given only phonemically regular words, that is words which follow a completely regular spelling pattern. In such words there is a one-to-one relationship between sounds and the letters by which they are recorded, for instance, monosyllabic short-o words. In words like *hop, box,* or *dot,* in every single instance the *o,* stands for the same sound. The child who now meets a new word, say *fox* or *log* or *mop,* will be able to decode it on his own, even if he has never been taught to read this particular word before.

Bloomfield's gigantic contribution lies in his reforms regarding the structure of the reading vocabulary. Unfortunately, he was so strongly opposed to a phonics approach that he would not allow any phonic elements in his teaching method. He and his followers were opposed to teaching the sound names of the letters of the alphabet and to any form of blending. Instead they insisted that the children be taught the alphabet names of the letters only.

In practice, a pure linguistic approach works as follows. The teacher puts the words *can, man, Dan, fan* on the board. She tells the children what the words say, and the children repeat the words after her. If they don't remember what a word says, they are to say the alphabet names of the letters. But reciting the alphabet names "cee aye en" is actually a handicap, because they do not lead the child to the spoken word [can]. In practice, a pure linguistic program does not allow for learning by insight unless a child is bright enough to make the transition from the alphabet names to the sound names of the letters on his own.

A fourth major approach to the teaching of reading is Structural Reading, a modified form of linguistics. It is linguistic because it presents only linguistically regular words in a highly structured sequence. It is modified because it insists on teaching the sound names of the letters of the alphabet as the easiest and most expedient tool in unlocking words. Teaching a child the sound names of the alphabet gives him the code in a way that allows for understanding and independent discovery. Also in such an approach, words are not taught as complete units. Instead, the teaching starts with an analysis of the spoken word into sensible parts and proceeds to the analysis of the structure of the corresponding printed word. In this way a child does not have to depend on the teacher to read aloud a new word, but he is able to decode words on his own.

The practice of teaching the sound names of the letters and of only presenting regular words is very much in accordance with conclusions drawn by Jeanne Chall, a professor of education at Harvard, who investigated a great many research studies on the beginning reader. "The best results," she says, "probably come from using some control of spelling patterns and directly teaching their sound values."[6]

A modified linguistic approach, such as Structural Reading, incorporates the valid features of existing teaching methods. It adopts from the phonics approach its theoretical premise that, in spite of its irregularities, English is a phonetic language. Since there exists a definite correlation between the sounds of speech and the letter-symbols that record them, a child must be taught this correlation as an indispensable tool in learning to read. It also incorporates the premise of the sight approach that comprehension must be the focal point of all reading instruction, that reading at sight must indeed be its goal. Finally, it uses the linguistic innovation of controlling the beginning vocabulary on the basis of spelling regularity as the easiest and most efficient way of teaching a child to decode.

The unique contribution of a modified linguistic approach to the teaching of reading is that it changes the dynamics of the learning process. The learning process is such that children can learn by insight into structure, apply their knowledge to new words, and correct their own errors. Early in the learning process they realize that reading does not allow guessing but requires genuine mental effort to arrive at the accurate decoding of the word.

[6] Chall, Jeanne S., *Learning to Read: The Great Debate* (New York: McGraw-Hill Book Co., 1967) p. 118.

Their comments show their understanding of what reading, at this initial stage, means.

Bobby, at the age of five, read the word *is* for the first time, on his own. Asked to use the word in a sentence, he pointed to his head with a whimsical grin and answered, "Reading *is* something you have to figure out up here."

At the very beginning of learning to decode Robin (5:4) guessed from the picture that the word said *man*. When I silently pointed to the word underneath the picture, Robin sounded it out, "Da-d. Dad! I thought it was a man from the picture, but it says Dad, so they mean Dad. I can read words. That is real reading!"

THE NATURAL READER

A little girl appeared at the door of her mother's study, stating firmly: "I want to have a reading lesson. *Now!* I want to learn to read." The mother, tired from a long day's work and not able to tune in so fast to her daughter's request, simply shook her head and said: "You will be five in three months. That's when we'll start. We don't start teaching reading in our family until children are five." The girl, ordinarily very amiable, insisted. Her mother refused with equal vehemence. Not until the girl sobbed bitterly: "But I want it now!" did the mother give in. The mother had been arbitrary and wrong. The child was ready and learned to read in less than six months.

The principal of a New York City school who was experimenting with the Structural Reading approach in two of her first grades consistently put off teaching her own son to read at home and promised that he would learn to read in school. After six weeks in first grade he came home one day and confronted her in a cold fury: "You promised me I would learn to read in first grade, and I am not learning! We talk about pictures! What about your promise?" She brought him the first Readiness Book of the Structural Reading Series[1] and explained the first pages. At seven o'clock the next morning she woke up to hear him working on the sound names of the letters. In less than two weeks the boy asked for the second Readiness Book, which he finished on his own. He demanded the third book in the series and worked phenomenally fast and with very little help went through it in less than a month. He was delighted about finally being able to read; his faith in his mother was restored, and no damage was done. But the mother herself felt that she had almost missed a crucial moment and, in retrospect, she realized that she probably should have started to teach him at four, when he was first interested.

From these two examples we can see that almost as crucial as *how* is the question of *when* a child should start learning to read. Here, too, the beleaguered parent is faced

[1] Catherine Stern, Toni S. Gould, and Margaret B. Stern. *We Discover Sounds and Letters.* Book A-1 of the Structural Reading Program. New York: Random House, 1972. This book systematically develops all the reading readiness skills, which are a prerequisite to learning to read. It also teaches ten letters by their sound names.

with conflicting advice. At one extreme are some experts in early education who are convinced that a child is not ready to master this complex skill until he is at least six years old. They warn parents not to make any attempt to teach their children at home. Wait, they say, once he's in school; the teacher, who knows best how to do it, will lead him gradually into reading. At the other extreme are books such as Glenn Doman's *How to Teach Your Baby to Read* that urge an early and energetic drill designed to produce an infant reader in every playpen.

Parents find themselves in a dilemma. If they wait and leave the actual teaching to the school, will their child, in a perhaps overcrowded class, run the risk of never learning to read, or at best, never enjoying it? Yet if they defy this position and go ahead and teach their preschooler, will they be interfering with his natural healthy development and possibly cause worse damage? As in so many other areas of child rearing, parents must often feel they are damned if they do and damned if they don't.

The Critical Period

It should be helpful to think about learning in general. It has been found that there are optimum times for children to progress intellectually and to develop basic skills. These have been referred to in the professional literature as "sensitive" or "critical" periods. Trying to teach a skill before the critical period is wasteful and often frustrating for both teacher and student. On the other hand, waiting beyond the critical period is unproductive because the child's natural aptitude for achievement and growth has subsided.

Now let us apply this concept of critical periods to the field of reading. The peak of interest for some children obviously occurs much earlier than the majority of our schools allow for. There are five-year-old children—and of these many first show interest at four—who are so curious about "what the words say," so eager to learn to read, that they cannot wait. There are natural readers, just as there are natural athletes, and you cannot postpone their learning arbitrarily until they have reached a certain chronological age when presumably they are ready to be taught in school.

It seems logical and necessary that the child who is fascinated by letters and words be taught when *he* is most eager to learn. Obviously the quality and quantity of learning will be greatest when he is most interested. The child who is a natural reader signals by his behavior that he is ready to learn to read. As a parent you can learn to assess his behavior. The natural reader shows many if not all of the following characteristics:

• The natural reader is very much aware of printed words. He notices the labels on cereal boxes and canned goods. While driving along the road he notices highway signs such as "Yield" and "Stop." When being read to he points to a word in the book and asks, "What does this word say?" Or, "Does this word say 'Mom'?"

• Many, but not all, natural readers seem to have a phenomenal memory for printed words. If told that this word says "cornflakes" on the cereal box, they remember it and, with great delight, read it every time they see it. Similarly they'll remember the "Stop" sign every time they pass it in the car. They'll recognize not only their own name in print but their friends' names as well.

• Many natural readers scribble constantly. In the literature they have been described as paper-and-pencil kids. They are always busy copying words such as the names of their friends or the days of the week. Their interest in the written language manifests itself by trying to master it through writing.

• Many natural readers show a high degree of persistence. They usually stick to an activity for a much longer time than do children of the same age. They go on long interest binges. It is delightful to observe these children totally immersed in an activity, unaware of distractions. Their concentration span obviously is a great asset in an early learning-to-read venture.

The question of *when* to teach a natural reader who shows all the signs of readiness still has to be answered. The critical period is marked by the signs just mentioned; but it is also contingent on the child's internal maturation.

Before a certain maturation, no matter how interested he seems, readiness skills may be developed, but the actual reading skill should not be taught.

While it is impossible to give a precise chronological age at which all natural readers should be taught, the following guidelines do exist.

Two- to Three-Year-Olds

Two-year-olds and three-year-olds are not ready to sit down and learn letters. They are intent on exploring themselves and the physical world, and they need all the opportunity they can get for sensory-motor development.

No matter how interested these children appear in written words, they should not be taught to deal with the written language, in letters or words, because they are not mature enough to make the connection between the concrete and the abstract. The observation that a child, until he is about four, cannot think abstractly is born out by the eminent Swiss psychologist, Jean Piaget.

Piaget has made an immense contribution to the difficult task of evaluating an individual child's readiness for learning by describing the successive stages in the young child's cognitive development. The two- or three-year-old can only react to the concrete situation; he cannot reason beyond what he sees. He is not capable of symbolic or abstract thinking. For instance, he cannot comprehend that a banana, an apple, an orange, so different in their appearance, have something in common: they belong to the group of things to eat. It follows that, in the field that concerns us here, reading readiness, a child cannot understand that different objects like *mitten, mask, mirror,* and *magazine,* have something in common: they belong to the group of words which start with the same initial sound [m]. Since the child, at two and three, is not able to think abstractly, specifically to classify, he is definitely not at a good age to learn the relationship between sounds and letters. His intelligence is not mature enough to learn that skill.

Children as young as two or three sometimes can be taught a letter of the alphabet; for instance they can learn mechanically, by rote, that the configuration *m* says [m]. Or they can be trained to respond to the printed word *toes* with the spoken word [toes], an approach advocated by Doman in his book, *How to Teach Your Baby to Read*. But such drill dulls rather than furthers the child's intellectual development. There is no excitement and no active participation in learning when learning consists of repeating what the parent has said. It is wiser not to teach reading to a two- or three-year-old; better postpone it until he can *understand* the learning process and is thus able to make independent discoveries like figuring out a letter's sound or reading new words on his own.

However, there are other areas in which a curious two- or three-year-old interested in language can be challenged. The most important is the *spoken*, not the written, language. At this age the young child is intent on learning new words and concepts, and he is very proud when he can use new and difficult words in his speech. As a parent you can help enrich his speaking vocabulary by talking to him, answering his questions, and explaining new words and concepts to him. The richer the child's vocabulary, the better you prepare him for reading, since his reading comprehension directly builds on his comprehension of the spoken language.

Reading aloud to a three-year-old can be a delight. After you have read a story, encourage your child to talk about it. At this stage he is able to develop auditory discrimination. He can learn that a spoken word begins with an initial sound that he can hear and identify. Games that develop auditory discrimination are fun for the young child and, at the same time, develop a necessary skill which has to be sufficiently practiced before a child can learn to read (for detailed description of these games, see chapter four).

Four- to Five-Year-Olds

This is the best time for a child who shows the signs of a natural reader to learn, provided he can be taught in such a way that he can understand the process and make his own discoveries rather than learn configurations by rote.

Giving him the go-ahead at this stage has tremendous advantages. We teach him when he is most interested in learning and has the maturity to learn.

The child gains a feeling of achievement and competency, something he needs to feel in *all* areas, not only in blockbuilding, paint, and clay, but also in cognitive areas such as learning to read, write, and do arithmetic.

Recently, psychologists interested in the development of the child's thought processes have stressed how important *early* learning experiences are in shaping the child's learning for the rest of his life. If he experiences early that he can deal successfully with symbols, he will develop a feeling of competence. The child who is aware of using his power of reasoning rather than his ability to repeat or memorize develops an image of himself as a thinker. This early feeling about himself, that he *can* deal with the written language, is crucial in his development as a learner.

By teaching him at his optimum time, his intrinsic motivation is constantly reinforced. Very little, if any, outside pushing from the adult is necessary. The enjoyment of learning for its own sake is the single most important outcome of teaching the child to read at this sensitive period.

Having accepted the idea that a child should learn to read at the critical period rather than later in first grade when he may have passed beyond it, you as a parent may ask: "Wouldn't it be better if my child, obviously a natural reader because of his compelling interest, picked up reading on his own? Is it a wise idea to interfere with this natural process?"

Some natural readers actually do try to teach themselves. If somewhere along the line they pick up enough phonics to figure out the code on their own, they can become excellent readers. However, it is risky to let a natural reader teach himself because, on his own, he may learn to guess.

Guessing comes naturally to children who are impatient, for it is always easier and quicker than accurate decoding. Such a child may read *String Beans* instead of *Whole Green Beans* on the frozen package in the freezer. Or on his way to his friend's house, he may read *Hill Street* instead of Hill Avenue. At this beginning level, when the child's guessing has no serious consequences, errors may slip by unnoticed. After all, the child will bring the package of beans to his mother and he will arrive at his friend's house. Yet guessing will seriously interfere with the child's learning in later years. For instance, it will prevent him from understanding the exact meaning of a paragraph in a history book or from solving a problem in mathematics books which require the accurate reading of every single word.

Breaking a habit of guessing that has been practiced for years is very difficult. Once your child thinks he can read, he will not be eager to relearn, either from you or from the teacher in school. At this point reading instruction loses its original flavor of excitement and takes on the taste of remedial teaching.

It is wiser if your child is taught to read correctly in the first place and that, at the beginning, he is taught sound-letter correspondence *before* he reads words. This way he has the tool which enables him to read each word accurately.

At the other extreme from the guesser is a natural reader who picks up a lot of phonics from an older sibling or friend and thus is able to sound out a great many words accurately. But he may not have any idea what some of these words mean. Although he may be able to call word after word in a sentence, he fails to get the meaning of the sentence as a whole. Such word calling is an equally faulty reading process which is also hard to unlearn.

There is another crucial reason why your child should be taught systematically rather than be allowed to teach himself haphazardly. Reading and writing both have their natural roots in the spoken language: the child should learn simultaneously how to transfer listening to reading and speaking to writing. Each reinforces the other. For instance, the practice of tracing a letter helps the child to discriminate letters and insures the identification of each letter.

Some natural readers between four and five lack the eye-hand coordination necessary for writing. It is especially important for them to be taught this skill along with reading. Children at this age never tire of the games aspect of an activity and, through playing, develop eye-hand coordination and soon the writing skill itself. In first grade, however, they find it a boring chore to learn to write the letters of the alphabet. After all, they already can read books!

Spelling, too, should be part of this learning process. Here we adults have to free ourselves of the notion that to spell a word means to be able to recite by rote the proper sequence of the alphabet names of the letters. Can the child only be said to spell the word *cat* if he recites the alphabet names of the letters "cee aye tee"? Such a performance bears no resemblance to the spoken word "cat." Think instead of spelling as a natural process which also has its roots in the spoken language. A child can say the name cat out loud and, listening to himself, can record the sounds he hears by their corresponding letters. (This presupposes that he has been taught the sound names of the letters.) A four- or five-year-old finds it intriguing that he can record a word he can pronounce, and in this way, spelling becomes a natural process of self-dictation at least in the beginning of instruction (see chapter nine).

The Parent as Teacher

Having accepted the idea that your child should be allowed to discover reading, writing, and spelling when he wants to, the question of who shall teach him has to be answered. If you live near a modified Montessori preschool (a school that includes in its program not only the teaching of the three R's but also allows for discoveries in the creative fields) or an enlightened public school kindergarten (a kindergarten that allows discoveries in reading, writing, and arithmetic, not only in the creative fields), send him there. Your child will learn to read at his own rate at that school, and you can use the suggestions in this book as enrichment activities to enhance your child's learning. If such a school is not available, then you yourself should help him with these first learning discoveries. Do not postpone it. You want to give your child a solid preparation which will enable him later to be successful in learning to read easily and accurately.

Don't think of this as a formal teaching assignment. Your task is to provide informally the proper learning environment for your child to make his first discoveries in reading. You can accomplish this only if you feel unpressured and concentrate on establishing a relaxed setting where you will use the games which are described in detail and in their logical sequence in Part II of this book. Consider it a pleasurable and leisurely experience that you and your child are sharing, not as a job to be tackled with grim determination according to a prescribed timetable of achievement. On the contrary, your goal is to keep his natural curiosity in reading and writing alive—not how much and how fast your child can learn.

Your child makes no distinction between learning and playing, at least not until he goes to school. And one advantage of helping him to read when he wants to learn is that he will regard it as play.

Now what happens to children who do learn to read early? Are they bored in first grade? On the contrary. First graders who already know how to read are able to start reading real books at a more advanced level, and naturally the more they read, the better they become. Early readers report, years later, how satisfying it had been to be able to read all the picture books in kindergarten, the birthday cards at parties, or the headlines in the daily newspaper. One first grader who found a letter in his desk from his mother who had visited his classroom on parents' day proudly refused the teacher's offer to read it to him as she would for the other children. "I already read it," he explained nonchalantly.

Research has shown that these early readers keep their headstart even after several years have elapsed. Dolores Durkin, now professor of education at the University of Illinois, has been conducting studies on children who learned to read before going to school. She has concluded that ". . . without coercion, young children—(four- and five-year olds) with IQ not being a strongly relevant factor —are able to learn to read, and those who learn early continue to read at a higher level than those who do not even after six years have elapsed."

Even more important than their headstart is the fact that the child feels competent and successful from the very minute he starts school. Nothing succeeds like success. It is an intoxicating inspiration and catalyst that helps establish a positive cycle; from learning to motivation to more learning and heightened eagerness to learn. Such a cycle is vitally important because it shapes the child's attitude toward learning, and this can influence his success throughout his school years. Its importance almost equals the actual accomplishment of the reading itself.

SHOULD *ALL* CHILDREN START EARLY?

"You'll have to teach Bobby to read *before* he goes to school," Mrs. B. told me on the telephone. He'll never learn once he's there. Here he is four-and-a-half and he won't sit down with a puzzle. He doesn't even want to listen to a story."

I knew Bobby's family, because I had tutored his two older brothers in reading. Both were above average in intelligence but had been handicapped by severe perceptual problems that gave them difficulties in school. I promised to take Bobby on a trial basis to find out if he was intellectually mature enough to learn to read. If Bobby's mother was right, it did seem sensible to give him a chance to learn to read *before* he encountered failure.

The mother's remark about her youngest turned out to be the understatement of the year. Bobby wouldn't listen, period. To any simple direction such as "Take a pencil," Bobby replied, "What?" It soon became obvious that this was his stock phrase. Every direction, expressed in simplest terms, was challenged by "What?" or "What did you say?" Even simple questions such as "Would you like a cookie?" or "Would you like some punch?" received the same response.

Bobby was a restless child, and during each lesson some time was spent retrieving pencils and toys which "accidentally" fell on the floor. His mind ambled, too; he'd suddenly wonder out loud what his mother or his brothers were doing at home and when they were coming to pick him up. But he soon got used to the structured hour, sitting down, listening, and playing games, and within a few weeks, he appeared much less restless during the hour. I gave him the Readiness Book. Bobby was thrilled to be working in a real book. He would ask for "my book" as soon as he came into the study, and he was very proud of being able to do several pages each time he came.

Simultaneously, we were playing a lot of games. There were little toys on the table, such as a mouse, a lion, and an ambulance. Underlying these games was a teaching purpose: Bobby was learning that every toy, every object has a name which starts with an initial sound that we can identify. Lion starts with a [l], tiger starts with a [t], fan starts with a [f], and so on. Bobby had to learn to listen to my directions carefully and to concentrate on their meanings. He also had to develop sufficient auditory discrimination to be able to identify the initial sound. In a word like lion, he had to learn to hear only the consonant sound [l] not the alphabet name, *el,* nor the consonant plus a vowel, such as [le]. Bobby mastered the skill of auditory discrimination in about eight weeks, a longer time than most children his age take, yet it was excellent progress considering his low level of concentration.

At this point I felt very confident that Bobby was going to learn to read, and that these lessons were, at the same time, helping him to learn to concentrate. Although he still responded to most directions with "What?" I no longer had to repeat them. I simply sat back and waited, and in a few minutes he would carry out the direction or answer the question. As Bobby's attention span notably lengthened with each visit, both pupil and teacher felt the glow of success.

Now Bobby was ready for the second stage of learning. He had to understand the concept that the spoken sounds we hear can be transcribed into letters. I showed Bobby a picture of a mask with the letter [m] embedded in it. He identified the picture as that of a mask. I explained that the dark lines superimposed on the mask form the letter *m,* recording the first sound heard in the word mask, that is [m].

Figure 3.1.
Letter picture of *m*ask for the letter *m*

Then I asked Bobby to say the name of the picture, mask, trace the blue lines with his finger, and say [m]. Bobby understood this assignment; he was delighted to be able to trace the *m*'s in his workbook. In the next lessons he learned the letters *f* and *l* in a similar manner. I placed the three other pictures with embedded letters in a rack on the table. When working in his workbook or playing new games using the written letters, Bobby could use these pictures as a reference. But when I removed them, he was unable to identify a single one of the three letters. The m by itself did not say [m] to him. Chapter eight will explain in detail how to use similar letter pictures with your own child.

My Waterloo had come. After seven sessions of trying both old and new techniques, Bobby still could not identify any of the three letters. It is true that some children at this age, especially those with either a poor visual memory or a severe perceptual problem, take a relatively long time learning the difference between f and l, since they "look alike" to them. But all the children I had taught up to this time had learned to identify the m after a fairly short time, since the m has a strikingly different configuration from the f and the l.

Clearly, Bobby and I were getting nowhere, so I phoned Mrs. B. and suggested waiting six months to a year before we resumed the lessons. Mrs. B. was most unhappy. "Bobby is counting on his lesson tomorrow; he looks forward to it. Won't you see him and explain to him yourself that he can't come until he is older?" I agreed to do this, but I suspect that Bobby's mother told him that this was going to be his last lesson.

I was confirmed in this thinking when Bobby marched into my study the next day. To my surprise he identified m, f, and l without a mistake, demanded to learn the name of the new letter on the next page, and then asked for "more letters."

Apparently Bobby had enjoyed the lessons in the past and was determined not to give them up. I realized that Bobby's increased eagerness was not the only reason for his success in mastering the four letters. The past lessons had laid a good foundation, but Bobby had needed more time, more practice, and more patience to develop the skill of discrimination than anything in my previous teaching experience had prepared me for.

Something else dawned on me. Bobby had not been able to make the transition from recognizing letters embedded in their meaningful context, the letter pictures, to identifying the letters themselves—to see the curious squiggle of lines in a letter like m and hear that it says [m]. Obviously Bobby had a severe perceptual problem and we were, fortunately, correcting it in its early stages.

The young children whom I had taught previously had made this transition without any difficulty; but Bobby needed more time than I had allowed to overcome his learning disabilities. What was working for us was his heightened motivation and his increasing ability to concentrate and to comprehend; now he could master a learning process for which he had not been ready before. When Bobby left, triumphant that he was coming back the following week and "all the time until I know how to read," he did seem to be a couple of inches taller!

The question many readers will ask is: Would Bobby have learned the letters more easily if he had waited until he was six years old? Certainly, there is always a strong temptation to claim that a child is "not ready." But when does a child like Bobby *become* ready? Does he grow ready by himself?

In every area of learning a child's ability to acquire a new skill is determined by both what goes on inside the child (maturation) and what is going on outside of him (environmental stimulation). Jerome Bruner, discussing early learning in general and not confining himself to reading readiness, states: "The idea of 'readiness' is a mischievous half-truth. It is a half-truth largely because it turns out that one teaches readiness or provides opportunities for its nurture, one does not simply wait for it. Readiness in these terms consists of mastery of those simpler skills that permit one to reach higher skills."[1]

So, too, in reading, readiness does not spurt forth by itself from a hidden well inside the child at a given age. It is the outcome of both the maturation of his nervous system and the stimulation he gets from the world around him. Nor is maturation in itself enough to overcome certain deficiencies or stumbling blocks in preparing the ground for learning. So, we must teach a child those "simpler skills" that will actively prepare him to learn to read

[1] Jerome S. Bruner. *Toward a Theory of Instruction.* Cambridge, Mass.: The Belknap Press, 1966, p. 29.

successfully. In a nutritive educational environment—with the proper teaching sequence and appropriate materials allowing for a child's gradual learning through understanding structure—a child's critical period will occur sooner than it would if the child had been left alone without any instruction. The task of the educator, parent, or teacher is to adapt his teaching to the child's level of learning so that the child, in the process of learning, will be prepared to tackle the progressively more difficult tasks that have to be learned. Viewed from this active concept of readiness, critical periods in a child's learning depend as much on the skill of the educator as they do on the unique interests of the child.

Bobby, who with his perceptual difficulties showed all of the immaturity of a much younger child, wasn't "ready" to learn to read but he needed my help to become ready. It was particularly important that Bobby, as a slow learner, have an early start, since he needed a great deal of time to develop all of the readiness skills. The structured situation of the lesson by itself did a lot for his readiness: since he enjoyed the games he learned to sit still and listen. As he gradually progressed in learning, he experienced a feeling of achievement, which in turn sparked his interest and his motivation to learn. Thus through playing and without any coercion he learned to learn, and in the process he became more mature.

At four-and-a-half, Bobby's interest in learning to identify letters was apparent even when his actual learning had temporarily slowed down almost to a standstill, because he had found playing games with me enjoyable. For instance, he enjoyed the letter-writing game which provided him with the necessary tracing practice; he never realized that he was practicing the same three letters. At six, or even at five, it would have taken Bobby just as long to learn the letters, but he would have become bored by the games and, worse, discouraged by his slow progress.

Since my experience with Bobby I repeatedly found that children with severe learning disabilities need a great deal more careful help than the usual child to develop the skills necessary for learning to read. Because their reading readiness needs a longer time to be developed, they especially need to be started early.

Robin, another pupil, also benefited from an early start. She was no better prepared for learning than Bobby when she was referred to me. My first two sessions with Robin showed that she was so restless that she could only concentrate on a single game or activity for five minutes; she had very poor visual discrimination; she showed a marked tendency to reversals in copying even the simplest design or trying to follow any indicated direction with her pencil; and her eye-hand coordination was very poor. It was impossible to determine if her constant "What?" was due to poor auditory discrimination or to poor listening habits. Actually, the question remained an academic one for ten months, for I had to repeat every direction because "she did not hear it."

But hidden beneath all of Robin's restlessness and inability to concentrate appeared a good analytic mind and a keen desire to learn. She paid more attention to a hard game than an easy one, so in the second lesson, I introduced the letter picture for the [m]. She was thrilled. "That's what Susan [her older sister] did last year!" However, it took Robin ten months to learn nine letters. Without the letter pictures many letters "looked alike" to her.

We played a great many writing and tracing games to help her get a kinesthetic feeling for the letters. We constantly thought up new games; for instance, she invented a telephone game in which, with the aid of a toy telephone, she would call me, announce that she had a package for me, and then deliver a *lion* in person. To make sure I realized I was getting the correct package, she would trace over the *l* on a prepared page, saying, "I brought you a lion, and so I am writing the *l* for you." As her interest increased during those ten months, her concentration span gradually lengthened.

Robin went away for the summer at the end of June. When she came back, she entered public school kindergarten and came to me twice a week as before. To my tremendous amazement Robin had not forgotten any of the nine letters she had learned the previous spring. She spent only three months learning the next fifteen letters, although she did not entirely master them and frequently had to check their names with their letter pictures. I

sensed that Robin was now very eager to get to "real reading." I expected Robin to progress slowly, in part because
she had not achieved mastery of all the letters. However,
this was not the case.

What makes Robin's record so fascinating is the complete discrepancy between her long, hard struggle in learning the letters—it took her thirteen months to learn the
sound-letter correspondence—and her amazing progress
once she discovered reading. Because she was not only
very impatient but also had a rather low opinion of herself, I let her teach herself a great deal more than would be
possible, for example, in a classroom situation. When her
impatience led her to glance at a picture and guess at the
word rather than take time out to decode it, all I had to do
was to point to the word to remind her to read it. I did
hardly any talking at this stage of her learning. Robin was
immensely pleased with herself, as the following excerpts
from her record show:

Robin (5:7) reads all the short-o words by transfer
without first saying the names of the pictures. Today, she
also read *job, cob,* and *Mom* in a separate booklet. "Now
I know how to read *Mom,*" she announced proudly. She
read *gift* by transfer, although she has not yet been taught
words ending in a final consonant blend.

Comments:

"I was going to say *fishing pole,* because I looked at
the picture. But then I read it. It says *rod.*"

"I would have said *cow,* but then I read it and I saw it
said *ox.*"

"I was going to say *pig,* but the word says *hog.*"

May 26 (5:8) "I was going to say *bed* but I read it. It
says *sick.* I bet he is sick, and he has the mumps, and his
cheeks will be like apples."

June 24 (5:9) The following comments show how much
she is thinking while she reads:

Reads *socks:* "Why doesn't it have an x on the end?"

Reads *beach:* "Why do they have an a? I don't hear an
[a]."

Reads *because* on her own: "I can read *because,* but I
can't write it. That's what's so funny."

Robin's comments show her steadily increasing confidence in her ability to read and transfer her skill to new words. She mastered the reading process by the beginning of first grade and her avid reading kept her ahead. Sometime after Robin went away for the summer—the summer before first grade—I received an exuberant letter from her mother. Robin was going to the library once a week, taking out ten or twelve books at a time and reading them to herself and her younger sister. Needless to say, the parents were thrilled with this reading explosion.

Just as in the case of Bobby, the first question which comes to mind is: would Robin have learned faster if we had waited until first grade to teach her the letters when she was "more mature"? In this case, the answer came from her first-grade teacher, who called after two months of school to say that she was surprised that Robin could read so fluently. It was puzzling that there was no sign of a perceptual problem in reading; whereas in arithmetic she had great difficulty. She could not learn the symbols. After two months she still reversed numbers and could not keep up with the class. The teacher also wondered why Robin listened attentively to directions whenever writing or reading were concerned, but did not listen to any directions involving arithmetic. I explained that, indeed, Robin had many learning problems; in particular a poor visual memory. It had taken two lessons a week to teach her how to read. I had not even been able to introduce number symbols.

If simple maturation had been the solution to Robin's problem, the learning of numbers would have occurred quickly in first grade. It did not. She needed the same preventive tutoring in arithmetic as she had been given in reading.

Bruce is another example of the benefits of an early start. The public school psychologist had found that Bruce's eye-hand coordination was poor: his inability to hold a pencil and to follow lines was evident. In all tests requiring sensory-motor coordination Bruce showed such immaturity that he was considered "not ready" for kindergarten.

The diagnosis was correct. Bruce was not ready. In fact,

I had never taught a pupil who literally could not manage to hold a pencil at the age of four-and-a-half. His directional sense was nil, and his attention span was poor. He refused to draw a line connecting two dots or to write his name. It seemed obvious to me that the gap between his verbal intelligence and his extremely poor motor performance should not be allowed to widen to the extent that he considered himself "hopeless" in that area.

In September we started working together once a week. Bruce needed a lot of additional games to practice tracing, the single most important activity to develop eye-hand coordination. (It is a fact that tracing is also important in helping to establish the right direction and to prevent reversals.) After five months of hard work Bruce was able to identify every single letter. However, he could not write any of them free-handedly, and I did not pressure him, because it was obvious how inadequate he felt about his lack of ability in that area. Instead, he would dictate to me which letters to write, and then he would trace my letters. Nine months after we had started working together Bruce volunteered that he would like to write the straight letters on his own. In that lesson he wrote *l, f,* and *m.* The magical moment had come: Bruce was "ready" to write letters!

From my own experience I have come to believe that *all* children would benefit from an earlier start. The natural reader, at one end of the continuum, while needing less time to learn, should be taught before he goes to school, when his readiness for learning is at a peak. At the other end of the continuum, children like Bobby, Robin and Bruce, with some kind of learning problems (which may actually be affecting the measured IQ), need an earlier, systematic development of skills necessary for learning to read *successfully.*

Left on their own, they would have reached their critical learning periods too late or never. At six they would not have the patience or interest to go through the slow learning process of mastering the letters. Through proper teaching their teachable moment was advanced; they had become interested in letters through playing.

It has been my experience that children with learning

difficulties need at least one, if not two, years to master the reading process. These two years are better spent *before* any formal learning takes place, i.e. before first grade, so we can insure that they do not feel the slightest discouragement.

Even under the best of teaching situations—an open classroom and a warm and supporting teacher—a child with learning problems easily feels frustrated. Even if he is allowed to progress at his own rate and follow his own interest, he is no longer interested in learning to identify five or six letters. He's bored. He feels that, being six, he should be able to read, and yet here he is struggling with the mastery of only six letters or, worse, unsuccessfully trying to remember the looks of as few as ten words. He feels discouraged about his own performance, and thus about himself, for he does not meet his own standards. Obviously, such negative feelings interfere with the learning he can do.

Given the premise that an early start is desirable for all children, with or without learning problems, within the normal IQ range, the question presents itself: who is going to provide the early start? Ideally, all public school kindergartens should be prepared to teach a structured readiness program to all children. In this way, natural readers could learn to read at their optimum "critical" times, and children with any learning difficulties could have all the learning time they need.

Unfortunately, many kindergarten teachers still do not teach such a structured readiness program. Often they are told not to on the theory that it is better to wait until the child's fine visual discrimination is more developed. This old-fashioned concept of readiness seems unnecessarily rigid. It prevents a five-year-old from learning, whereby moving slowly and building on his interest, he can be encouraged to successfully compensate for his disability.

If your local kindergarten does not provide a structured readiness program and you can not find a preschool that will teach your child sound-letter relationships, you yourself should get him started by teaching him some of the letters by their sound. Don't push your child; let him learn through games at his own pace. Your aim is to give him enough familiarity with sound-letter relationships that he won't feel pressured and perhaps threatened by failure when he arrives in first grade.

How much your child learns is unimportant. The point is to give him a painless introduction to the process of learning. The child who has learned the sound names of even six letters will have an easier time in first grade than one who has not begun the learning process.

Learning letters takes time. Unlike all other previous pre-school experiences, letters go in one definite direction. A cat's identity is the same whether it is sitting, standing, running, or facing to the right or to the left; but if a *b* faces to the left, it is a *d*! It takes a long time for some children to develop this sense of direction, to develop auditory or visual discrimination, or to acquire better eye-hand coordination. Yet if he has not mastered these skills in his pre-school period, he will have outgrown an interest in achieving them. For instance, a four-year-old is interested in holding a pencil and being able to write a letter of the alphabet. He is proud of his achievement that he can record a sound he hears by a symbol he has just learned. A six-year-old is no longer fascinated by such baby stuff. He wants to write stories. Yet he, too, has to start at the beginning.

My plea for an early start for *all* children is not made because I feel that they could not learn to read later. It stems from the conviction that a child should enter school with a fair chance that he will feel competent from the beginning. His success in school helps establish a positive cycle and inevitably brings enjoyment in learning. The satisfaction of achievement is in itself enough to make him want to try hard to learn more. But the child who feels inadequate loses his courage, and his motivation to do well decreases rapidly. Nowadays, especially, the young child meeting difficulties is likely to think of himself as stupid and, therefore, a failure right from the beginning of his schooling.

The importance of the early years in the development of a child's personality is a well-known and accepted fact. Only fairly recently has increasing recognition been given to the importance of the early years in his cognitive development. Concretely, he must be given stimulation and tools for learning. Psychologically, he must acquire early the feeling of "I can" in the intellectual area. Successful experiences of intellectual competence have a direct influence on the child's feelings about himself, and this is probably the most important single reason for wanting all children to have the chance for an early start in learning to read.

THE ARGUMENT AGAINST TEACHING THE ABC

The most important reading readiness skill your preschool child develops is his ability to identify letters by their sound names. He should never be given the job of memorizing the alphabet, which at this stage is simply a meaningless exercise; rather he should be allowed to discover the letters in their natural, intelligible relationship to the sounds heard in words. In this way he learns to use his inductive reasoning, an indispensable tool for all future learning.

A whole generation of parents brought up on the ABC song may well ask: "Why not teach the ABCs?" We all know how proud a four-year-old is when he can sing: "Now I know my ABCs." Knowing the alphabet is a concrete achievement that most children enjoy, and it gives their parents the false sense that their little ones are forging ahead. But whatever the temptation, don't teach it.

The preschool child is fascinated by the written language. But telling him that a given letter M says [em] means nothing to him. Modern psychologists, such as Piaget, have shown that the young child can only understand a concept when it is presented on the concrete level. Before learning letters he must first understand that the concrete object, such as a mitten, has a name, and that this name starts with a [m] before he can grasp the idea that this sound [m] is recorded by the symbol m. Only by moving from the concrete to the abstract can the child eventually grasp the fact that these strange squiggles on paper, which you call letters, record sounds heard in words he himself uses every day. This genuine insight into the relationship between the concrete and the abstract, between sound and symbol, is crucial. True understanding of symbolic abstractions, in contrast to rote knowledge of the ABC, represents a gigantic step forward in your child's intellectual development, as Jeanne Chall and other educators have pointed out.[1]

There is another good reason not to teach the ABCs. My experience has shown over and over again that knowing alphabet names can be an actual handicap. When reading the word *dog* for the first time, a child should be able to

[1] Jeanne S. Chall, *Learning to Read: The Great Debate.* New York: McGraw-Hill Book Co., 1967, p. 159

sound out the word [dog] and realize what it means: "a dog." But he can sound the word only if he knows the sound names of the letters. Merely naming the letters [dee oh gee] does not enable him to arrive at the word [dog].

Most four- and five-year-olds readily accept the explanation that every letter has two names: a sound name and an alphabet name, which are pronounced differently. For example, when we pronounce the word *f*an, we hear that it starts with a [f] sound. That we call the sound name of the letter; you hear only the pure consonant, you do not hear a vowel sound attached to it. The alphabet name [ef] has a completely different sound. Children readily accept the suggestion that learning the sound names of the letters is what we need both in learning to read and spell. They enjoy the idea that letters, just like people, have two names: the sound names are the "first names" and the alphabet names are their "last names." They are amused with the analogy that letters, like children, should be called by their first names and not by their last names.

The Bobby you met in chapter three, who was attending a kindergarten where the alphabet names of the letters were taught, expressed the difference very succinctly: "When I come here, we better never use the last names of the letters. They don't get you to read. When I come here, we better stick to the first names."

Grown-ups are harder to convince of this order of priority. Perhaps they are so accustomed to using only alphabet names that they see this knowledge of the ABC as more useful than it is. They see the alphabet as a simple lesson in memorization which, like counting, they can certainly undertake to teach their children themselves.

Eric, a remedial student of mine, came across the word *on* in his book. He kept staring at the word and saying: ō en. But saying ō en did not help him to decode this simple word. Systematically, he had to unlearn using the alphabet names of the letters before he could learn to read using a decoding process.

Michael, a second grade remedial pupil, had been taught only the alphabet names of the letters in school. When he was confronted with a word he didn't know he said helplessly: "Double u e? Double u e? Which word is it?" Knowing the sound name of the *w* might well have been sufficient clue for him to be able to decode the simple word *we*.

Even the mature reader does not use the alphabet names of the letters in reading. Let us assume that you, the adult reader, came across a word in a newspaper clipping that you did not know. In such a case do you say to yourself: "aitch oh em oh tee ay ex eye ess?" I don't think so. Instead you sound out the word: ho-mo-tax-is. Looking up a word in the dictionary is a later skill, and that skill is facilitated by knowing the sequence of the alphabet.

In contrast, children who know the sound names of the letters and who are given insight into the structure of words possess a basic tool for figuring out a great many words on their own. Examples of this transfer have occurred in many New York City first grades, with children ranging in ability from slow to very bright. These children were able to read words like *has, mad, sad,* and *ran* on their own before they were taught these words.

Knowing the sound names of the letters is equally effective when it comes to spelling. If spelling is taught not through rote memorization, but through an analysis and understanding of the structure of words, then the knowledge of the alphabet names again proves to be not only wasteful but actually detrimental to learning. I have many records of bright first graders who came to me for help knowing only the alphabet names of the letters. When asked to complete *ca* to the word *cat*, they said cat to themselves, emphasizing the final [t], as I had shown them, and then looked up and asked: "What shall I write, ce, em, or pe?" The sound [t] did not automatically make them think of the letter *t*, which they only knew by its alphabet name tē.

The roots of spelling, like those of reading, lie in the spoken language. A child who has mastered sound-letter correspondence does not need to learn to spell through memorizing an unrelated sequence of letters which is an extra burden on his memory. He knows how to spell the word *hat*, because he listens to himself say: *h a t*. He should not be expected to produce an automatic response to the word's alphabet names, because he does not *hear* aitch ā te. The word *hat*, furthermore, is a linguistically regular word: he can clearly hear each individual sound.

Then he can record these sounds, naturally and logically, by their letters, *provided he knows the sound names of the letters.*

In this instance, it is the *adult* who has to unlearn. He has to free himself from the traditional concept that learning to spell requires being able to recite the alphabet names. We should not accept such a narrow definition of spelling. The vast majority of children are taught spelling by the rote memorization of the sequence of letter names: Jay ū em pe spells jump. Children who learn to spell this way have to memorize the sequence of hundreds of letter names as if they were so many different zip codes. The zip code 03741 has no meaningful relation to the place where you live. Neither do the sequence of the letters jay ū em pe bear a meaningful relation to the whole spoken word jump. Children who are taught spelling this way miss out on the exciting discovery that spelling, like reading, has as its base spoken language and is a logical recording of sounds heard in the spoken word.

Thinking ahead to the time when your child will be learning other languages, there is another, unexpected advantage to knowing the sound names of the letters: this knowledge provides the child with a key not only to learning to read and spell in English but in many foreign languages as well. A child who can readily use the consonant sounds can also later apply this learning. For example, knowing that the letter says [f] helps him in sounding out not only *father* but also *frère, fuente,* and *Frau* in French, Spanish, and German respectively. Merely knowing that the letter says *ef* is of no earthly use in learning to read and spell in any language.

Ideally, letters should be taught as recorded *sounds* of spoken words, for speech precedes reading. The sound must be taught first; its transfer to a symbol abstraction is a second step.

Discovering the sound names of each letter, which will be discussed in detail in chapter eight, is a learning process that makes sense to the child. The first step involves the identification of initial sounds: What is the first sound you hear when I say *mitten?* You hear a [m], not an [em]. What is the first sound you hear in *fan?* You hear a [f], not an [ef]. Only when this skill is acquired should the child learn to record the sound he hears by its corresponding letter. If the spoken word is represented by a picture of a mask with the letter m superimposed on it, the child by himself can learn to infer that since the picture is that of a mask, the letter must say the initial sound of mask which is [m]. Learning letters through his own deductive reasoning, a form of self-teaching, in fact, gives more impact than if you, the parent, provide the abstraction.

It is, therefore, important to resist the temptation to start your introduction of letters by pointing to a *printed* letter (or a felt, sandpaper, or magnetic letter) and telling the child the alphabet name of the letter. Instead, you start with the spoken word and help him discover that every word he speaks starts with an initial *sound*. After he can identify all the letters by their sound names, and only after this, do you have the option to then teach him the ABCs. He needs these in order to acquire the grown-up conventional way of identifying letters, but not because this name serves any real function in learning to read and spell. Children who have good inventory memories learn the last names of the letters easily, and it does not then interfere with reading and spelling.

But there are children who have poor inventory memories and who have enough difficulty just learning the correspondence between each letter and its sound name. Some children, like Bobby mentioned in chapter three, have difficulty with intrasensory transfer. It is hard for them to *hear* the [m] and then point to the visual form m. These children should not be introduced to a second auditory form of each letter, especially since they still have to learn a second visual form, i.e. the capital form of each letter, to be able to read sentences and proper names. It is essential that children with any of these learning difficulties not be burdened with learning the alphabet names of the letters at a time when such knowledge is ornamental rather than functional. In these cases it is always advisable to leave the teaching of the ABCs to the school.

When should these children who have poor inventory memories learn the traditional alphabet? A child who learns to read systematically through decoding only linguistically regular words like *cat, pin,* and *mop* needs to learn the alphabet names of the vowels before he comes to the decoding of words like *cāne* or *pīne,* where we use the alphabet names of the vowels in reading. He does not need to know the alphabet names of the other letters. Sometime, perhaps only in third grade, when he can read and write fluently, he can be taught the alphabet names of the letters both as a means of communication (no child wants to go through life referring to the letter *m* as [m]!) and as an aide to acquiring dictionary skills.

How to Help Your Child to Spell

Even if your child knows the alphabet names of the letters, don't ask him to spell words orally. Have him write down the word. In this way he is spared countless hours of memorizing spelling words—literally a lifesaver for all those children who may be bright but who have poor rote memories. Even an irregular word has some relation to the spoken language; for instance, the word *night* has a correspondence between sounds and letters at the beginning and end; the child need only to remember that it contains a silent *gh* in the middle which make the preceding vowel long. This is easier to learn than to commit the entire word, letter by letter, to memory.

How to Help Your Child to Write His Name

Over the past twenty years I have come across countless children, some as young as three, who print their names in all capital letters. In fact, capital letters are taught in most kindergartens on the ground that capitals are easier to print than lowercase letters and are all of the same height, whereas lowercase letters vary in size. But many children who have written their name in all capitals while they are in kindergarten find it incredibly difficult to break this habit in first grade, as any first grade teacher will testify.

So if your child asks you to write his name for him, give him an exact model of how he would do it later on, for example: *Bobby.*

If your child asks you how to write his name, let him first trace your model with his finger. Show him where to start. Watch him. You don't want to take the chance that on his own he might just trace his name backward. Such a habit is hard to break. Now let him go over his name with a crayon or a pencil. Unobtrusively dot his name on all of his drawings or collages and have him trace your model.

Teaching Your Child Lowercase Letters

In chapter eight you will also find out how to teach your four-year-old child to write letters. You will be teaching him lowercase letters only. Why? We do not use capital letters in writing except at the beginning of a proper name or the beginning of the first word in a sentence. Thus, the letters your child writes most often will be lower case. Only if your child consistently practices lowercase letters will he eventually find it easy to write words in lowercase only. This way he will not write words interspersing lowercase letters with capital letters.

Admittedly, lower case letters are more difficult. But by being introduced to them first, your child has more opportunity to practice them as much as he needs to through tracing games he enjoys. In this connection it would be helpful if alphabet books, games, and educational television programs, such as the otherwise excellent "Sesame Street," would teach the lowercase form of the letters and the sound names rather than the alphabet names of the letters.

The arguments against teaching capital letters before lowercase and against using the ABCs will make sense to you if you realize that you, as an adult, do not usually write words in capital letters. Nor do you make use of the ABCs in reading. So why teach them to a child who is just venturing into reading and writing? It will only conflict with his learning.

BUILDING FOUNDATIONS: TOYS, PLAY, AND READING ALOUD

Your baby starts to learn from the time of his birth, and you play an important part in these early learning experiences. You may not realize it, but from the very beginning your warm relationship and enjoyment of your child encourages him to learn.

The importance of the parent's role cannot be overemphasized. One research study[1] has found that the difference between early readers and nonreaders lies not so much in the children but in the parents. The parents of nonreaders usually have little or no time for their children, and, interestingly, are much more willing to accept the school's suggestion that they leave the teaching of reading and writing to the school. The research shows that parents of early readers generally enjoy playing with their children. They find the time to talk to them, to answer and ask questions, and last but not least, to read to them.

You can build a secure foundation for reading in your child by actively enriching his early years and by being sensitive and attuned to his critical periods of interest and capability. Even in his first months you influence his ability to learn. By fostering his curiosity and the acuteness of his five senses, you are giving him the first stepping stones to learning. In the first year of your baby's life there is material you can provide to stimulate his awareness. This is hard to believe, but the time you give and the games you play develop his readiness for learning.

For instance, the young baby learning to focus his eyes will be interested in the slight movement of a mobile attached to his crib or playpen. He learns to follow moving objects with his eyes. In the same way he learns to follow the rattle that he holds as you diaper and dress him. This is the very beginning of the development of concentration, essential to all learning.

Toddlers learning to walk are soon running in all directions. "He is into everything," the weary mother complains. But in the course of his active explorations, your toddler will voluntarily sit down and "work" hard at some object he has discovered. He may have found your pots and pans and try very hard to fit a lid on a pot. Or he may have come across your percolator. While taking it apart,

[1] Dolores Durkin, Children Who Read Early—Two Longitudinal Studies. New York: Teachers College Press, 1966, pp. 95–96

possibly trying to put it back together again, there appears on his face an expression of deep concentration. Respect its appearance because the development of that concentration is one of the most important steps in preparing your child for reading. From his earliest years, encourage him to develop and extend his natural periods of concentration and involvement. Don't interrupt. Understand the importance of his absorption even if he takes the percolator apart.

Educational Toys and Activities for the Two- to Three-Year-Old

As your child gets older give him some educational toys: toys that have a built-in task to be solved, such as arranging brightly colored rings in a given order, from the smallest to the largest. Mariann Winick, in her book *Before the 3 R's*,[2] gives innumerable suggestions about how to make your own educational games with very little cost.

If you buy commercial toys, be sure they have an educational function, a task that the child can understand and solve; for instance, a box with cut-out geometric slots so that a circle will only fit into a circle. A simple jigsaw puzzle with just a few pieces is very useful, especially if you work it with him. However, as explained in chapters four and eight, don't give him magnetic letters or toys bearing the alphabet with the idea of teaching him their names.

Try to restrict the number of toys. Too many interfere with concentration. There should be a favorite object or two, a good educational toy, and a puzzle within reach at any given time so the child has the chance to work and play without too much disorganization. This way he can enjoy the absorption of a task and then the feeling of success at having completed it. Success generates success. The satisfaction: "It fits! I have done it!" will spur him on to further efforts.

Be sure not to overlook the importance of such large muscle activities as catching and rolling a large ball, balancing on a line or crack without slipping off, and learn-

[2] Winick, Mariann P. *Before the 3 R's*. New York: David McKay Company, 1973

ing to skip and to use playground equipment. Finding ways that your child can practice these activities as the development of gross motor coordination are very essential to learning to read. It precedes the development of eye-hand coordination, which is the next necessary step.

When you observe your youngster trying to place pegs in holes or making his first scribbles, be sure he has crayons, paper, blunt kindergarten scissors, and old magazines at his disposal. Cutting out pictures and making "drawings" develop eye-hand coordination. What is important is the fact that he is holding a crayon and using both his eye and his hand to guide it. The drawing that he produces is immaterial. Young children sometimes are eager to start "writing," but don't encourage this, because he may teach himself letters incorrectly, and as discussed in chapters three and four, the only learning sequence that allows for discovery involves sounds first and letters later. As a parent you can encourage the development of his eye-hand coordination by showing him a particular skill or activity a few times and then letting him practice on his own. For instance, let him struggle with his socks even though it may take a lot longer than if you helped him; or let him feed himself in spite of the inevitable mess. Here, too, the feelings of achievement and competence eventually contribute to the formal learning process.

Letting Your Child Help Around the House

You can encourage your toddler's independence by letting him help you around the house. When he has finished a meal, show him how to put first his cup then his plate (unbreakable, I suggest) in the sink. It will develop his motor coordination to climb on the chair, to reach the sink—with his cup in his hand—and it will do great things for his self-esteem to be considered old enough to help you.

When your child is about two-and-a-half—some start at two and some will only be interested at three—you can let him do more. He can, for instance, help dust, wash spoons, pour milk (yes, it will spill at first), or wipe a tablecloth. If he makes a mess, ignore it. Don't measure his job against any standards, but thank him for his helpfulness. What matters is that you allow him to sense his growing competence through his independence.

As the two of you work around the house, talk to him about the jobs you are doing. By asking questions and answering him, you will help develop his speech and his comprehension.

Helping Your Child Develop Language

You have the most dramatic role in the development of your child's speech. Once he has reached the point of physiological maturation where he is able to talk, the response and encouragement of the people around him makes an enormous difference in how fast and accurately he learns to express himself. If you show delight at every new word or sentence your child can say, you encourage him to develop, at his own rate, his oral language skills.

Pronounce clearly the name of each object he points to; he will soon copy you. Don't correct his sentence structure or pronunciation when he is trying to tell you something important; his first need is communication, not correction. Do it later, if necessary, perhaps in the form of a game. Always speak to him distinctly and carefully and in complete sentences. You are his model, and he'll copy your ways of talking.

At the same time that he is expanding his vocabulary, let him learn new concepts from you. Help him to identify colors or to use numbers—on the spoken, concrete level— or to name objects in categories, such as food, toys, clothes. This ability to classify is a prerequisite for learning to read.

Enlarging Your Child's World

Family trips and even small excursions are important ways of enlarging your child's world. Take him with you whenever you can: not just trips to the playground and the supermarket but to the zoo, aquarium, subway, or airport. As early as eighteen months your child will enjoy these outings and so will you, provided you help him accept certain limits such as holding onto your hand when necessary. Talk to him as you venture forth. Your observations about these new places help to enrich his speaking vocabulary. More questions on the child's part indicate that he is ready for more answers; he becomes familiar with and verbal about areas he may later meet in books. The more direct verbal interchange your child has, as Dr. Burton L. White, Director of Harvard's Pre-School Project, points out, "the better off he is in comparison to watching and listening to television."[3]

T.V. and Early Learning

At this point something has to be said about television. There is no doubt that television helps children by enriching their speaking vocabulary, particularly those whose families are not able to do so. But television will never be a substitute for live interaction, and on the whole, it makes for passive listeners. Selected good television programs, such as "Sesame Street" and "The Electric Company" or shows about animals, are outstanding exceptions; yet even watching the good programs must be supervised judiciously so that a child does not become passively glued to the set.

Some parents say, "Look how well my child can concentrate. He sits for hours watching T.V." This kind of activity does not count as mental effort and concentration. Such children's minds are not really at work; they are being hypnotically acted upon.

Using television to enrich rather than stultify is one of the most difficult tasks that parents have. From the very beginning you rather than your child must be in control of the television. Get him used to the fact that two or three favorite programs is all you allow, no matter how big a temper tantrum he can throw. Don't use the television as a baby sitter.

Within these set limits you have the option of ameliorating the bad effects of T.V. Watch a good program *with* your child. Together you might enjoy a show about wild animals. You can ask and answer questions about a specific happening, thus sharpening your child's observation. In this way watching T.V. becomes a shared experience, one that imperceptibly requires a more active watching on the part of your child. If you are present when your child picks up a word or an idea from T.V. without really knowing what it means, he can talk it over with you and learn what the terminology or the concept means.

[3] Burton L. White, *The First Three Years of Life.* Englewood Cliffs, N.J.: Prentice Hall, Inc., 1975, p. 160

Watching T.V. together, however, can never be a substitute for reading to your child or playing games with him, both of which lengthen his attention span and develop his ability to concentrate.

Reading Aloud to Your Child

While enriching your child's world don't overlook the fact that looking at books and being read to is one of the best preparations for learning to read to oneself. A toddler who of his own volition sits down with a book may do so because he is imitating his older siblings and parents, but he may also become genuinely fascinated. In the beginning it is better to choose reality-oriented rather than fantasy books: picture books with simple, uncluttered illustrations of objects or animals to identify, such as *Winter Noisy Book* by Margaret Wise Brown and *The Snowy Day* by Ezra Jack Keats. (See Appendix VI for other books to read aloud to your child.) Then a simple story like *The Three Little Pigs* takes the step from identifying pictures to identifying situations. And he can learn to turn the pages by himself.

Sitting close to you physically at reading time enables him to absorb through a kind of psychological osmosis your own understanding, humor, and warmth. He will catch your love of books, your enjoyment of a good story, and your appreciation of good illustrations. Last but by no means least, he will cherish the special bond between you that grows from sharing books.

The child who has been used to regular or frequent reading time will be ready to progress from picture books to nursery rhymes and story books between the ages of two and three. As he grows older, the books you read aloud can become more difficult in keeping up with his rapidly developing understanding of the world around him. On the reading-aloud level you can stay ahead of his chronological age, often ahead of the recommended age set by librarians, which is usually based on the child's ability to read to himself. You can, therefore, tackle books that would be much too hard were he to try to read them to himself.

How you read is important: that is, your emphasis, your tone of voice, whether or not you are patronizing. Your way of reading may well become the model of how the child himself will later read. If you yourself are really paying attention to what is happening in the story of *Barbar* or *Madeline* or *Mr. Rabbit and the Lovely Present*, your child's imagination and his sense of humor will also catch fire. As you read aloud, his feeling for animals and people in the story, his understanding of himself, and his relation to others will grow.

Children naturally thrive on their parents' warm attention during the story time spent together. Their speaking vocabulary is enlarged by making the connection between words and pictures. The child gets used to sitting quietly and paying attention. Soon you can make simple suggestions: "Show me the horse. Show me the cow." Now he takes the next step and points them out. Later you can ask him questions: "Who found the ball? Where did they live? What did you see when you went to the zoo?"

As your child gets older, ask more difficult questions which will teach him to interpret the story. Get him to identify the main character, to describe the sequence of events or the cause and effect between people and events. Occasionally, your child may like to make up his own ending to the story. By responding to your questions he will develop his imagination and reasoning ability.

All of these skills must be developed and practiced orally before a child is able to use them in terms of the written language. This preparation is essential. Just as speech precedes reading, full use and comprehension of the *spoken* language must precede that of the *written* language.

There are young children who when you read to them point to certain words in the book asking: "Does this word say 'Babar'?" or "Which word says 'Daddy'?" It is also true that some children, at a very early age, pick out certain letters whose shapes and patterns they like and are delighted with their ability to recognize a particular letter wherever it occurs. While these children should be given the proper answer—the name of the word and the sound name of the letter (not its alphabet name!) I would not take these questions as a signal to teach them reading. Three (or two) is *not* the optimum time for teaching a youngster reading. As has been said, he is too young to grasp symbolic abstractions.

The age of three is, however, the best time for developing specific readiness skills. Enlarging the speaking vocabulary and gaining facility in using language, both as a means of communication and as a way of expressing throughts, are the important gains for this age and must precede learning printed symbols. A three-year-old child has so many questions to ask, and the parent's job is to answer them precisely. Today's children are smarter earlier than former generations were because of the increased complexity and stimulation of the world around them. But the ability to actively absorb, organize, and understand what he has perceived requires the help of the parent.

READINESS GAMES FOR
THE THREE-YEAR-OLD

Playing games offers you a unique opportunity to help your child develop many specific readiness skills essential for his success in learning to read. While the readiness skills do not follow a strict 1–2–3 order, there exists a general sequence in the child's ability to master them which you should follow. For instance, a child *first* has to learn to identify objects or pictures by their proper names, to observe details in a picture. Only *after* he has learned these skills is he able to develop an understanding of what *sequence* or *classifying* means.

Following is an overview of all the readiness skills divided for the sake of convenience according to age groups. The purpose of this particular breakdown is to show you that each major building block rests on the completion of the preceding one and is not to suggest the exact age at which a child should start to develop certain skills.

The Three-Year-Old
Should be encouraged to develop his ability:

- to listen
- to expand his speaking vocabulary
- to concentrate
- to observe, e.g. to select a given object in a picture
- to follow directions
- to develop eye-hand coordination, e.g. to guide a pencil
- to follow a prescribed direction, learning left-to-right progression

The Three-And-a-Half to Four-Year-Old (Chapter Seven)
Should be encouraged to develop his ability:

- to understand sequence
- to classify
- to develop fine auditory discrimination, specifically to identify initial sounds of spoken words

The Four to Four-and-a-Half Year Old (Chapter Eight)
Should be encouraged to develop his ability:

- to understand sound-letter correspondence
- to develop fine visual discrimination, specifically to identify letters

Let us see what the three-year-old's skills involve:

To Listen
You have already encouraged this ability in your toddler when you got him used to listening to you. The child who learns to enjoy listening to a story is prepared well for "listening" to an author tell a story, i.e. for reading.

To Expand the Child's Speaking Vocabulary
Speech precedes writing. A child has to know what a lemon or what a tiger is, to give but two examples, before he can understand their written counterparts. The child who has a good command of the spoken language, who is encouraged to learn new terms and concepts, will comprehend their meaning in print.

To Concentrate
A child who is capable of focusing on a task, of shutting out all distracting outside stimuli, is prepared for all learning, not just reading.

To Observe—to Select a Given Object in a Picture
This readiness skill is a prerequisite for the development of finer visual discrimination, which is required in the identification of letters. The child who can pick out a picture in a book after listening to the description of its main characteristics will eventually learn to discriminate between pictures which differ only slightly. Gradually his visual discrimination sharpens, so that he will be able to identify the different letters.

To Follow Directions
A child must develop the skill of following oral directions before he can follow written directions.

To Develop Eye-Hand Coordination, to Guide a Pencil

Eye-hand coordination is an essential reading readiness skill which you already helped to develop earlier when you provided your two-year-old with thick crayons and paper. However, since most two-year-olds are independent and want to do everything by themselves, two is not the best age to show your child how to hold a crayon.

Around three, he may well be eager to imitate how you hold a crayon, especially if you tell him that you have a new game for him where he needs to know how to hold a pencil the right way. Once your child can hold a thick crayon reasonably firmly, try the tracing and drawing activities suggested later in this chapter. Be patient. It takes time for him to learn to put the crayon down at a starting point, to go along a prescribed path, and to stop at the end. Some children need a great deal of practice before they develop the proper eye-hand coordination. Their eyes see the path, but the hand cannot steer the crayon in that direction. Your task is to stick to the games aspect of the activity. Don't set yourself a goal for how soon your child should be adept at guiding a pencil.

To Develop a Directional Sense; Learning Left-to-Right Progression

Developing a directional sense is also an important reading readiness skill. The activities suggested later teach your child to move in a prescribed direction. Thus he carries out directional tasks on the concrete level as a preparation to the later introduction of the terms "right" and "left." It is not advisable at this time to teach your child the terms right and left; there is time for teaching him these names when he is five or six, after he has developed a directional sense.

It has been my experience that a great many children need a very long time—sometimes one to two years—to develop this directional sense; yet it has to be learned, since reading requires the ability to move the eyes in one direction only: from left to right.

All of these readiness skills can be developed by playing games. Although it is impossible to give you an exact time schedule for starting these games, it is vital to the child's success as a learner that he experience early, around three, the feelings of competence and confidence that come with completing a specific task. These experiences help to lay the foundation for reading readiness. He wants to *learn*, because he enjoys the resultant feeling of mastery.

Take your child's behavior as a signal for which games to try. If he enjoys following oral directions such as "Please, put these spoons on the table," he is probably ready for listening games such as *Do What The Puppet Does* or the *Command Game*. If he is constantly scribbling with a pencil or a crayon, try the games *Follow the Arrow With Your Pencil* or *Put In What Is Missing*.

Here is a list of games to use as a source for suggestions rather than as a rigid agenda. Don't play more than one or two games a day. What is most important is that you and your child should enjoy playing together. Many of these games lend themselves well to group games, birthday parties, or family outings. Some of the games are adapted from Maria Montessori, who used them to develop certain readiness skills in the preschooler.

Games Developing Listening Skill and Concentration

I. Listening Game

Ask your youngster to close his eyes. He must tell you what noises he hears from the street and who makes them: the honking of a car, people talking, the rustling of leaves, the chirping of birds, the barking of a dog.

II. What Made the Noise?

Place several objects on a small table, such as a pencil, a spoon, a glass, a pot, paper, a wooden spoon. Ask your youngster to close his eyes. Make a noise by tapping the pencil against the table and ask him how you made the noise. Or ring the spoon against the glass, or later, the wooden spoon against the pot. Or rustle the paper.

III. Tapping a Rhythm

Tap simple rhythms on a drum or with a wooden spoon on a pot and ask your child to repeat it. Start with no more than two or three taps, so that the child will be successful when he tries to imitate you.

IV. Where Is the Alarm Clock?

Take a small alarm clock that ticks noticeably and hide it. Your child should find it by trying to track down the ticking. After a while, you can make the game more difficult by extending your realm to two rooms.

Games Expanding Speaking Vocabulary

V. Riddle Game

Say, for instance, "I am thinking of something you wear on Halloween. You wear it over your face."... Or "I am thinking of something Dad wears in bad weather. He wears them on his feet."

VI. Rhyming Game

You can easily explain what rhyming means from the nursery rhymes your child knows. Ask if "cap" and "nap" rhyme. Or say: "I think of something that rhymes with fat. It is an animal that meows."

Games Developing Observational Skill and Concentration

VII. I See Something

The child who is trailing behind you while you are trying to get the house ready for company may enjoy a dustcloth of his own to help you, but he may also like to play this game. You start out by saying: "I see something that is red, and it is in this room." The child will guess various objects and finally hit on the right one. If necessary, help him by giving an additional clue, e.g. "You can sit on it." Inevitably, the child will want his turn to give you a riddle.

VIII. Grab Bag Game

Put three or four toys or objects in a grab bag. They must be of different shapes and sizes, for instance, a ball, a comb, a doll, and a spoon. Ask your child to close his eyes, reach into the grab bag, and get hold of one object. He is to feel the object and tell you what he has in his hands without looking at it. He can then check if he is right.

Again the game can be adjusted and made easier if the child watches and sees which objects you put in the bag, or it can be made harder if he has no idea of what is in the bag.

IX. Match the Color

Put four spools of different colored threads on your tray. Place four identical spools in a nearby room or on a table far removed from your tray. Ask your child to choose one of the spools on your tray, look at it closely, and name its color (you must help him if necessary). Now he should put the spool down, go to the place where the matching spools are placed, and pick the same color without looking back at your tray. He then brings the spool to you to check if it is the same as the one he originally chose on your tray.

X. What Did I Take Away?

Hiding games are splendid for lengthening the child's ability to concentrate and developing his powers of observation and resourcefulness.

Put four objects or toys on a tray. Ask your child to enumerate them; then ask him to close his eyes. Take one of the objects away and ask: "What did I take away?"

You can make this more difficult by using five objects. Or while your child's eyes are closed, take one toy away and put a new one in its place. Now ask: "What did I take away and what new toy did I put in its place?"

XI. Where Is the Thimble?

Hide the thimble in one room; then call your youngster and ask him to find it. If you notice that he is getting discouraged, give him helpful hints: "You are getting warmer."

XII. Which Cup Has the Toy?

Put four paper cups on a tray. The cups must be exactly alike. Hide a small toy, e.g. a little fish, under one of the cups while your child watches you. Now move the cups around, always moving two cups at a time. Let go of those two cups and move two different cups. The child's eyes must stay glued to the cup where the toy is hidden. Finally, stop and ask him to point to the cup where the toy is hidden.

XIII. Find the Picture

Choose a picture book that has very clear, uncluttered illustrations. Have the child sit opposite to you so he can't see the picture you are looking at. Describe what you see: "I see a man on a horse; in the back are a rooster and some hens." Now close the book, hand it to your youngster, and have him find the picture. Here, too, there is a progression from easy to difficult, if you first choose a book your youngster knows and eventually take a book he does not know. In the above example, the task is easy if it is the only page that has a man on a horse. It is hard if there are several pages showing a man on a horse, but only one where a rooster and hens are in the background.

Games Developing Skill of Following Directions

XIV. Stop When the Music Stops

On the piano play a simple tune, or tap a rhythm on a drum or other object. At times play very softly, so the child has to listen very attentively. The child is to walk to the music. But the instant you stop, the child has to stop in whatever position he finds himself. He cannot even take half a step.

Your four- or five-year-old may want to learn to skip to the music. Teach him to skip slowly, showing him in slow steps how he alternates lifting his feet. Then he can skip to the music. Again he has to stop when the music stops. This time he is allowed to bring his foot down to the floor.

XV. Do What the Puppet Does

Hold a puppet or a doll in your hands, facing you as your child does. When you make the puppet jump up and down, your child must imitate him exactly. When your puppet lifts his left arm, or right foot, so must your child, and so on. This game is also fun to play with more than one youngster.

While the young child enjoys the challenge of obeying these directions, these games are also helpful in developing a directional sense. Asking the child to move in a prescribed direction is an excellent preparation for learning the terms "right" and "left." Learning to read requires a strongly developed directional sense of being able to move from left to right, for reading proceeds in one direction only: from left to right.

XVI. Command Game

This is a marvelous reading readiness game which not only develops the ability to listen well but trains the child to remember a sequence of verbal commands. You begin by asking your child if he would like to play the command game. (If he says "no," do it some other time, for example, when he has company and they have run out of ideas.) Then say: "Listen carefully. I want you to bring me a spoon from the kitchen, then I want you to close the door to the bedroom, and then I want you to sit down on the floor, right in front of me." The child must follow your "commands" in the exact order in which you have given them. Obviously, you can make the game simpler by giving only two commands at first or harder by giving eventually four commands. Five or six commands make the task challenging for any five-year-old.

Games Developing Eye-Hand Coordination and a Directional Sense

XVII. Follow the Arrow

With chalk, draw a large circle on the kitchen floor. Tell your child he must walk exactly on the chalk line. Next draw an arrow alongside the circle: your child must walk in the direction of the arrow. Erase the arrow, and draw another arrow pointing in the opposite direction. Let your child trace over your line with chalk.

You can combine this game with one previously mentioned: have the child stop walking the instant you stop tapping the drum.

This is a good game to play in the sand on the beach, with more than one child, or out on the sidewalk.

XVIII. Follow the Arrow with Your Pencil

Draw a faint line across a sheet of paper. Now place an

arrow above the line, at the left, to indicate to your child that he should cover your line with his pencil in the prescribed direction, from left to right.

This activity develops eye-hand coordination and a directional sense as well as dexterity in using a pencil.

You can make this activity more interesting by cutting out pictures or drawing pictures that have a sensible connection (see figure 6.1).

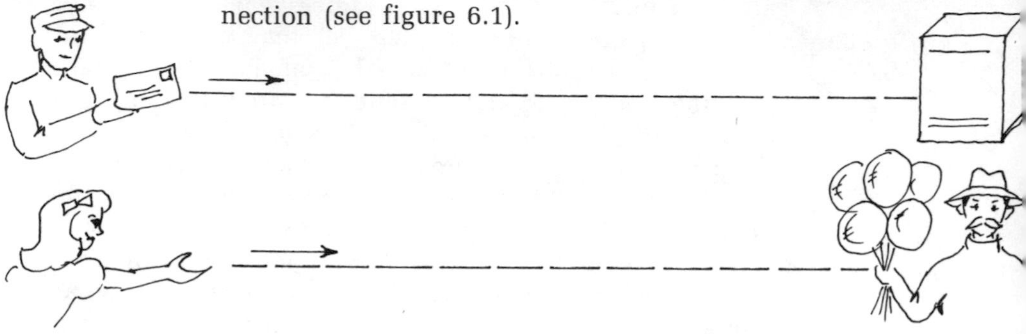

Figure 6.1.
Follow the arrow with your pencil.

This variation then also provides an opportunity for enriching your child's speaking vocabulary, for he can make up a story about each set of drawings.

XIX. Finish the Drawing

Draw a series of incomplete circles, squares, and triangles. Place an arrow next to the dotted line indicating to your child that he should trace the line in the prescribed direction. Completing a circle is a good preparation for writing letters that have curves.

Going from row to row let your child identify the two geometric figures which are alike. This develops his observation, simultaneously providing him with practice for developing eye-hand coordination and directional sense. If he wants to he can even learn the names of the geometric figures. Also, he can color the two figures which are alike.

XX. Put In What Is Missing

Make very simple drawings leaving out an important item. The game is for your child to figure out what is missing and to draw it in.

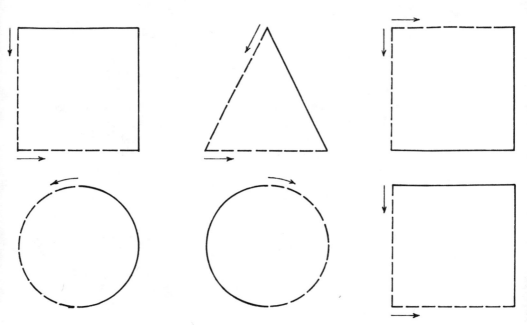

Figure 6.2.
Finish the drawing.

Suggestions: a face without a mouth, a doll with one leg,
a bicycle with one tire, and so on.

Figure 6.3.
Put in what is missing.

In conclusion, it is important to stress that the time in
your child's life *when* you consciously start nurturing general reading readiness is inextricably tied in with *how* you
start and with the emotional and intellectual atmosphere
around the child. The home environment should be the
"good earth" from which all learning flows.

Learning to listen attentively, for instance, is possible
for the child who has been given relatively few commands, and these in a firm, friendly voice which he re-
spects and has learned to hear. The child who is shouted
at constantly tunes out the grown-up and may later

transfer this unwillingness to listen to his teachers.

It is necessary to have clearly defined rules in daily living, to give your child the security of knowing what to expect and who he is. The very young child has to accept brushing his teeth as inevitable, even on days when he does not feel like it or when he is too tired. But learning and intellectual curiosity are different from the routines and habits your child has to acquire. The desire to learn springs creatively from the child's natural curiosity: it cannot be forced. Avoid a head-on collision over any activity related to books and learning. If you do not discipline him in these matters, he'll keep the feeling that learning is exciting and rewarding in itself.

READINESS GAMES FOR THE FOUR-YEAR-OLD

Before you go on with the games described in this chapter, it is advisable to assess how well your child has mastered the games presented in chapter six. For an informal evaluation of his progress, use the games described in chapter six. If he can do them easily, he has the foundation to develop the skills that we will be dealing with here. If he cannot do them, continue playing the games described in chapter six for another month or two until he masters them.

To Understand Sequence

Understanding that events happen sequentially is an important reading readiness skill because, on the spoken level, sounds occur sequentially: in the word [man] you hear the sounds [m] and [ǎ] [n] in that order. Correspondingly, on the written level the letters have a sequential order.

To Classify

Seeing different objects as belonging to a common category is a challenge to the child's intelligence. As a matter of fact, it was tested in the early intelligence tests. It can and should be developed in the four- or five-year-old. Most four-year-olds enjoy this new way of looking at objects. A spoon, knife, and fork, although they have different names and look different visually, all belong to the category of eating utensils. Later the child will apply this ability to spoken words: mitten, milk, mirror, although they mean completely different things, all begin with a [m] sound.

To Develop Fine Auditory Discrimination; Specifically to Identify Initial Sounds of Spoken Words

This skill must be mastered before going on to the next two skills. The child must be able to *hear* the initial sound of man before he sees the corresponding letter m.

The games that follow will help develop the readiness skills described. All of these games present a definite task to be mastered. Thus they present a challenge to your child and are not boring to you.

Developing these readiness skills can only be done in a

relaxed play milieu which is enjoyable to you and your child. Your child will look forward to this opportunity of having you to himself. Try to set aside a definite time of day, either early in the morning or after supper, so that the child can count on his uninterrupted play time. Fifteen or twenty minutes a day should be enough. Naturally, it is not a good idea to choose a time when your child is likely to want to go out and play with his friends or, worse, when he is already involved in play.

There will be occasions when you cannot find the time for playing these games. Don't let that worry you. The necessary skills for learning to read can be developed in spite of occasional interruptions. While playing any of the readiness or reading games, make sure that you always sit alongside your child, never across from him.

The following list of suggested games and activities is not intended as a rigid agenda. Look at it as a resource file for you to draw on. It is more important that you both enjoy playing the games than that you be concerned about how many games are played each day. Choose one of the appropriate games and then, if your child wants more, you should try a second one.

As we have said previously, eye-hand coordination and a directional sense take many months to develop. Here are some more sophisticated tracing games designed to interest the four-year-old and to help him in this area.

Games Reviewing Eye-Hand Coordination and a Directional Sense

Your child must be able to hold a pencil and draw lines before going on to writing letters. Hopefully your child has developed some fine motor control with the tracing games described in chapter six. It is equally essential that your child has learned to move in a prescribed direction before he starts learning letters. Since these skills need constant refinement, more tracing activities are suggested in this chapter.

I. Follow the Arrow

Make the tracing activities more challenging by requiring longer lines. Be sure your child knows that they have to be drawn in a prescribed direction (see figure 7.1).

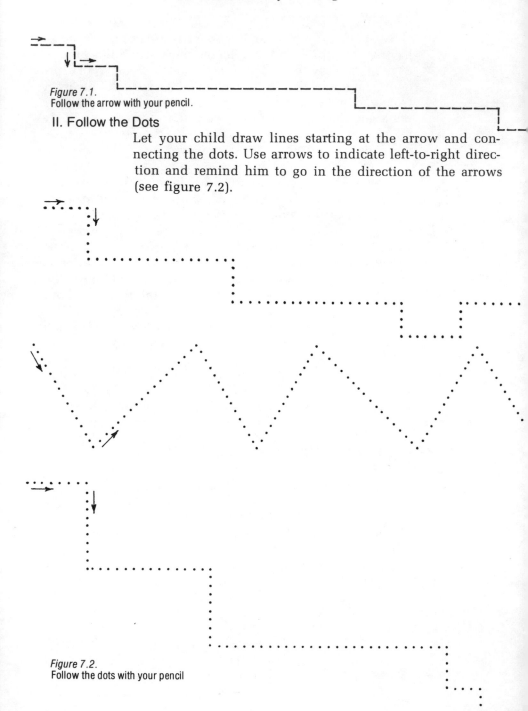

Figure 7.1.
Follow the arrow with your pencil.

II. Follow the Dots

Let your child draw lines starting at the arrow and connecting the dots. Use arrows to indicate left-to-right direction and remind him to go in the direction of the arrows (see figure 7.2).

Figure 7.2.
Follow the dots with your pencil

If your child shows a tendency to go in the opposite direction, play one tracing game each day, so that he gradually develops a sense of direction. Use the appropriate games outlined in chapter six.

A directional sense is crucial in learning to read. Yet few experiences in the preschool child's life help him to develop this skill. Learning to identify and write letters also requires this directional skill. This is difficult for the preschool child, for nothing in his previous unstructured experiences have made him aware of direction. The child has drawn a cat looking right or left, standing or lying down, and the grown-ups agreed it was still a cat. But if he draws a b facing the opposite way, he is wrong: it is no longer a b but a d, even though the two letters are identical except for the direction in which they face.

The same holds true in identifying a letter. When the young child correctly identifies a table or a chair even though it is lying upside down, when he recognizes tableness or chairness in spite of a shape or perspective that is new to him, we think he's highly intelligent. But when later he identifies a w as m he is wrong even though the shape is so similar.

Some children take a very long time to develop a directional sense. Yet it should be developed—at least to some degree—before a child learns sound-letter correspondence and before he learns to read.

Games Developing the Ability to Classify
III. Which of These Toys Belong Together?

Form a collection of inexpensive toys and objects, for example, a lion, a tiger, a mouse, and a fork. Ask your child: "Which of these toys belong together?" Help him to realize that the toys are all animals, but that the fork as an eating utensil is different. Now put a knife, fork, spoon, and a book on the tray. Which things go together? Which does not belong in the group? What are the objects called? Turning it into a game, put a miscellaneous collection of objects on a table nearby. Now put three animals on your tray and ask your child to find something on the table that will fit into the category (toy mouse or toy lion, for instance).

IV. What Does Not Belong?

Put five toys on a tray and one article of clothing, perhaps a mitten. Ask your child to look at the things on your tray and to take off the object that does not belong. If he responds correctly by taking off the mitten, ask him to tell you which category (toys or things to play with) the objects on your tray belong to.

Or you can play the same game by using pictures cut from magazines and pasted on large index cards. You can make the game more intriguing by using more subtle categories—e.g. you can have pictures of four children playing and one sleeping. Ask, "Which picture does not belong?" The child would remove the picture of the sleeping child and state the category: children who play.

As you collect more pictures, reverse roles and let your child choose the category and put you to the test.

Games Developing an Understanding of Sequence

Understanding sequence is an important readiness skill. In order to read a child must be able to sound out a word according to the sequence of the letters, and in order to write he must record in sequence the sounds he hears. Later he must be able to grasp the sequence of a story to be a good reader.

V. Which Comes First?

To play a sequence game, draw or cut out pictures that tell a story, e.g. show the picture of a cake mix and the picture of a finished cake. Put both pictures in front of your child and ask him to place the pictures in order from left to right. Which comes first?

You can make the task more difficult by using three or four pictures which have a logical sequence. First, place the pictures in their proper sequence and have your child tell the story they portray. Then scramble the pictures and have your child arrange them in their logical sequence. Suggestions: 1) Snow falling, a child dragging a sled out of doors, pulling it uphill, sledding downhill. 2) A child in bed, getting dressed, having breakfast, taking a school bus, sitting in kindergarten room.

Animals make natural sequence stories and, incidentally, offer information about nature.

egg	chick	hen
moth	spinning cocoon	butterfly
bee	beehive	honey
beaver	collecting twigs	building a dam

The most important part in the systematic development of reading readiness will be to help your child discover the correspondence of sounds and letters. This teaching falls naturally into two parts: first, identifying initial sounds of familiar words; second, the recording of these sounds by letters. In twenty years of teaching, I have found that it is important to teach auditory discrimination first. Many sound games should be played before the child learns how these sounds are recorded by letters. Hence in this chapter only games developing auditory discrimination are described. No written letters will be introduced as yet. Only after the child has mastered the skill of auditory discrimination will he learn (in chapter eight) how these sounds are recorded by letters.

Games Developing Auditory Discrimination

Not overlooking the possibility that some children are ready to play these games at three-and-a-half, I recommend that parents start these games no later than four. Since the games involve concrete objects and toys, most four-year-olds enjoy playing them. Some children need a great deal of time to develop this auditory discrimination.

Below are listed a number of games to help your child develop auditory discrimination, specifically the skill of identifying the initial sound of words familiar to him. Occasionally, a child may give the alphabet name of the letter even in these sound games. Remind him to *listen* to the initial sound. He himself will realize that he does not hear the alphabet name at the beginning of spoken words.

I. What Do I Want?

On a tray put a number of objects starting with different sounds like a *m*itten, a *c*andle, a *f*eather, and an *a*pple. Name each object, emphasizing the initial sound. (You hear the short sound of [ă] not its long sound [ā]). Now tell your child you are going to ask him to pick up the object you want from the tray. You won't say its full name but will call for the object by the sound that starts its name. For instance, you would say, "The name of the thing I want begins with [f]." Your child must pick up the feather.

II. Riddle Game with Pictures

For this game choose a book with pictures of clearly illustrated objects. Hand the book to your child and ask him to find the animal you can ride on. Its name starts with [h]. Or ask him to show you an animal that barks. Its name starts with [d].

III. I See Something

This is a new version of an old favorite. For instance, say: "I see something. You sit on it. Its name starts with [ch]." Some time later encourage your child to think up a riddle of his own.

IV. I Think of Something

This is a harder version of the riddle game—a good game to play in the car. Say, for instance, "I am thinking of something that you can see only in the sky, and its name begins with [m]." The child must think through that moon, sun, or stars would fit the first part of the riddle but only moon fits both specifications.

V. Command Game with Initial Sounds

"Go up to the bathroom and get me something that starts with [s]. . . . Then go to the desk and get me the [b] that is lying there. . . . Then go to the cupboard and get something to eat that starts with [c]."

VI. What Did I Take Away?

Collect several toys and objects in a plastic bag. At first, use only things whose names start with the sounds[m], [f], and [l]. Now, for, instance put the mirror, magnet, fork, and feather on a tray. Ask your child to lift up each object, one at a time, say its name, and see if he can tell you the very first sound the name starts with. Repeat after him the name mirror, for example, emphasizing strongly its initial sound, so your child can hear the sound better. Now ask him to close his eyes while you take one object away. Let us suppose you took the magnet away. When he opens his eyes, ask him to tell you what you removed. He will miss the magnet. Then encourage him to explain what the magnet is used for and to say its first sound.

VII. The Partners Game

Put three objects on the tray, two of them starting with the same sound, one of them not. Have your child pick out the partners. For instance, lion and lollipop start with [l], fork does not. An older child will want to reverse roles.

VIII. Which Toy Does Not Belong?

Put on a tray three or four toys, objects, or pictures of objects all starting with the same sound, and one extra which does not. For instance, put a mirror, marble, magnet, and feather on the tray. The child will pick out the feather as not belonging.

Once you used this classifying game for sound indentification, you cannot use it anymore for classifying games, because its correct task is to master initial sounds.

IX. Find Pictures

This game and the next one are harder and thus perhaps more suitable for five-year-olds.

Give your child a magazine or a mail-order catalogue, and ask him to find (and later cut out) pictures which start with [m]. Later ask for pictures whose names start with [f], and still later with [l].

X. Tell a Story

Tell a simple story leaving out the nouns, except for their initial sounds. For instance, Denise woke up in the m——. The s—— was shining. She put on her d——. As you go along, the child supplies the missing noun. Give him additional hints if he needs them. When the child is able to hear and identify the initial sounds of almost any word, then he is ready to learn the sound names of the letters.

Suppose your child can play these games effortlessly, i.e. he is really able to hear and identify the initial sound of any word. At this point you have to decide whether your child is ready for the next step, the recording of these sounds by letters. How will you know if your child has reached the "critical" or "sensitive" period for dealing with symbolic abstractions? The next chapter will tell you.

Special Suggestions for Children with Difficulties: Special Help for Developing Eye-Hand Coordination

Some children, at four, find it extremely difficult to do tracing activities. Some have to begin by learning how to hold a crayon. Let him study the position of your fingers when you hold one and have him copy you.

Some children find it difficult to guide the crayon with their eyes. Being able to start at a designated point and end at another is difficult for them and takes time and practice. You can simplify the tracing activity by omitting the arrow, having a very heavy starting line, and a strong heavy dot to mark the finish Maybe you can make a raised beginning with clay and a raised end if you think that feeling the beginning and end would help.

Special Help for Developing a Directional Sense

There are children who require a long time to develop a directional sense. They consistently draw lines from right to left even though the starting line is marked. They need to overlearn in this area. If you have a child who has difficulties with tracing in a prescribed direction, draw a chalk line on the kitchen floor. Use a basket or a chair as the agreed-upon starting point. At the end of the line put a little toy. At your signal the child has to walk on the line starting at the basket or chair, proceeding to the toy. He may then pick up the toy and keep it. He will want to play again!

Next give your child practice in tracing dotted lines from left to right. Mark the starting point with a heavy red line. Draw or cut pictures that will create a meaningful relationship between start and finish. Examples are:

Figure 7.3.
Follow the dotted line.

Do not use terms *left* and *right*. Do not teach your child which is his right or left hand or foot. This will only confuse him. Your aim is to get your child used to the idea that he is to move in only *one* direction which is prescribed. For this goal he does not need to know that he is, in fact, always moving from left to right.

Special Help in Developing Auditory Discrimination

Some children need special help in developing auditory discrimination. If your child has difficulty hearing and understanding that mitten begins with [m], follow these steps:

step 1: Tell your child that mitten begins with the sound [m], that man begins with [m]. Use as many examples of words beginning with [m] as are necessary for him to hear the [m] sound.

step 2: Sit your child opposite you to play a new game with you. Put on a tray only toys whose names start with [m]. Your child chooses a toy and says its name. Tell him your hand will go up to signal *stop*. When he sees your hand signal, he must stop saying the word. Raise your hand the minute your child says the [m] sound in mitten or man. By only using words which start with [m] your child will catch on.

step 3: Now use the other games described in this chapter which develop auditory discrimination, but use only toys whose names start with [m]. Once your child can identify the initial sound for these toys, use the same steps in helping your child hear the initial sound [f]. Now use only toys whose names start with [f].

step 4: Now use toys starting with both the [m] and the [f] sounds. If your child can identify the initial sounds of their names, you have helped him enormously.

Proceed in this way very slowly, introducing each new sound by only using toys—later pictures—with the new sound. Simplify the task by using only the new sound and the preceding sound that your child has just learned. At the end of chapter eight you'll find the sequence in which to teach letters; use the same sequence in teaching sounds now.

If you find that in spite of this extra practice your child has difficulties in any one of these areas, stop working with him temporarily. At this point I suggest a thorough checkup.

1. Have your child's hearing, vision, and speech checked. Ask your pediatrician where to take him. Usually a child has outgrown his baby speech by the age of four, so it is wise to have his enunciation checked at this stage as well.
2. Get an outside psychological evaluation by a psychologist or pediatrician who believes in early intervention rather than in passive waiting for eventual readiness to occur.

Don't keep on going if there is no progress, because your child will sense your apprehension and this is more detrimental than a postponement of learning. It may be that the psychologist suggests outside tutoring to help your child overcome his difficulties. Outside help is more advantageously used now than later after your child experiences difficulties in school. The vast majority of four-year-olds who have learning disabilities in a given area can learn a given skill if they are given enough time and practice, provided the help is given before they develop feelings of discouragement and failure. But you and your child need outside help. Suggestions for what kind of help is available are given in chapters ten and eleven.

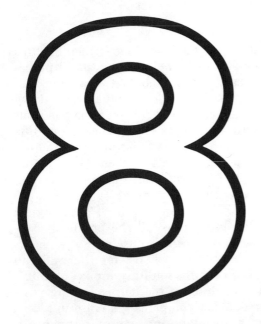

DISCOVERING LETTERS AS RECORDED SOUNDS

Helping your child discover the sound-letter relationships will be an exciting adventure for both of you. In all probability your child has been curious about the written language for quite some time. He may have evidenced this by scribbling on paper and then telling you what he has written. But now you will help him to progress from this make-believe activity to the reality of learning that the letter m, for example, represents the sound he hears at the beginning of monkey and mitten. The squiggle on paper, i.e. a specific letter, now says something!

To make this step two things are required: neurological maturation and the development of all the previous reading readiness skills we have been discussing.

Neurological maturation is necessary for the brain to make the connection between the auditory input of the initial sound and the visual input of the corresponding written letter. A common analogy compares the brain to a central switchboard in the telephone system: the brain connects auditory and visual stimuli registering the connection. The child is able to realize that the sound [m] he hears at the beginning of man is recorded by the letter m. Or that the letter m represents the sound [m] heard at the beginning of words like mitten and mask.

Recalling the list of readiness skills at the start of chapter six, the child now has two more skills to master.

To Understand Sound-Letter Correspondence

Understanding sound-letter correspondence requires a complicated learning process. Some children need a very long time, up to seven or eight months, to initially understand this correspondence.

To Develop Fine Visual Discrimination, Specifically to Identify Letters

To many children letters like l and f look very much alike; it takes them a long time, up to nine or ten months, to be able to pick out the critical features of all the letters.

When to Introduce Sounds and Letters

Even if your child is exceptionally bright, disregard those books that recommend teaching reading to two-year-olds.

Don't even teach your three-year-old letters of the alphabet. He is not neurologically mature enough to understand their meaning nor has he mastered the readiness skills necessary for learning to read. The age of three is the optimum age for playing the readiness games outlined in chapter six.

In a good learning environment most four-and-a-half and even four-year-olds, on the other hand, have mastered all the necessary readiness skills and have matured to the point where they can understand sound-letter correspondence. Also at this age they show an avid interest in the written language. Start your approximately four-year-old with one of the following games that teach sound-letter correspondence at a leisurely pace. Observe your child. If he does not want to stop as soon as he starts but asks to play more of these games, he is ready for this new phase of learning. If the game seems too hard and your child does not understand, stop. You can always try a few months later.

Once your child goes to kindergarten, find out if he will be taught the sound names of the letters there. If not, start him now on the games which let him discover sounds and letters. Natural readers should not wait beyond five, for they easily pass their "critical period." Neither should children with poor visual discrimination or perceptual problems start after five. They need at least one full year to learn some of the letters, and they should learn them before they enter first grade, as slowly as they need to.

Some children, like Bobby and Robin, need an extraordinarily long time, eight to ten months, to learn the critical features of one letter and distinguish them from those of another. These children do not, by some form of magic, develop this ability when they enter first grade. It must be developed early, at a time when there is neither pressure nor anxiety about learning.

Don't be concerned how fast your child learns in this area. The number of letters a child learns before he goes to first grade is unimportant. What matters is the child's understanding of the relationship between sounds and letters. If he knows only six initial sounds and their corresponding letters, he has already mastered a crucial readiness skill.

Sequence of Letters

At the end of this chapter we will give you a model of the size of each letter the child writes. We will also show you how to start writing each letter by accentuating the starting point. You will also find the sequence in which to teach the letters. (See figures 8.4 and 8.5.) Because we do not use the traditional alphabetical sequence, your child will not fall into the habit of blindly reciting the ABCs. We chose our sequence of letters on the basis of ease in auditory discrimination. The [m] the [f], the [l] and the [a] are the first four letters taught, because the child can easily distinguish between their sounds. In contrast, the [m] and the [n] which follow each other in the alphabet sound similar and are harder to distinguish; therefore, they should be separated by several other letters.

Letter Picture Cards

Each letter is first introduced with its letter picture card. This is the single most important teaching device throughout the process of learning letters. Through the device of a letter picture the learning of each letter makes sense to your child. The letter is embedded in the picture. As the child says the name of that picture, he identifies its initial sound and then can deduce on his own what the letter, on top of the picture, says. Using the spoken word as a starting point creates a meaningful relationship between sound and letter.

The letter picture card is a self-teaching device. If your child is unsure about a letter, all he has to do is find its letter picture card and say its name. By identifying its initial sound he finds the sound name of the letter.

Toys and Pictures

For practicing sound-letter correspondence you will use toys, pictures, and picture card games. As your child progresses you may want to rely more on pictures than on toys. Early on a child may become fascinated with the card games, described in the following section, in preference to all other games.

Games Developing Sound-Letter Knowledge

Following is a list of games to help your child understand sound-letter correspondence; they can be adapted to any letter or letters. We will start out with these four: m, f, l, a. When your child has mastered them, you should go on to preparing for the next four (see end of chapter for letter sequence). To play these games you need to do three things:

1. Here is how you make your own letter picture cards.[1] Choose a picture whose name starts with the sound you

Figure 8.1.
Letter pictures for m, f, l, and a

[1] See appendix for commercially available materials.

want to teach. Let's say you have drawn or cut out a picture of a mitten; paste it on a 5 x 8 index card. Then write with a blue magic marker the letter m in lowercase on top of the picture, 1¼" tall (see figure 8.1). The picture should be in outline form, preferably in black, so the letter stands out in the foreground (for samples see figure 8.2).

As you prepare letter picture cards for subsequent letters keep in mind that there is a difference in height between letters. Please use only the following sizes:

1¼" :m a s c n i r o e u v w x z
1¾" :p g j q y
2"   :f l t h b k d

2. Collect objects or toys whose names start with the sounds you are going to teach your child. At the end of this chapter you will also find suggestions on which toys or objects to use.

3. To prepare for card games, cut a number of 3 x 5 index cards in half. Look for similar size and for realistic pictures in catalogs and magazines (mail order catalogs provide a wealth of pictures), and paste one picture on each half of the index card. You need five different pictures for every sound you are going to teach.

In addition you need to write five plain letters on the same size card (one half of a 3 x 5 index card) to correspond to the five pictures you have selected for each letter. For instance, write five ms for the five m-pictures, such as mouse, mailman, mirror, magnet, and marble. Use the same size as you did for the letter picture cards. Always write the vowels in red and the consonants in blue.

Expanding Your Child's Vocabulary

Some of the objects or pictures suggested at the end of the chapter may well be unfamiliar to your child. I have purposely included such objects as a *ferry* or an *ambulance* to enrich your child's speaking vocabulary and broaden his knowledge. Identify each object, and talk about its use. Through such discussions his terminology will grow more precise; for instance, if he can't distinguish between a mitten and a glove, you can help him understand the difference.

Introducing the Letter *m*

Put the letter picture for *m* before your child. He'll identify the picture as a *mitten*. Now slowly tracing with your finger the blue lines of the letter, explain that these lines form the letter which says [m], the first sound he hears in mitten. Let your child trace the letter with his finger. Be sure he starts at the top of the letter and proceeds to trace it in the correct direction, from left to right.

I. Pick Out the Correct Toys

Place the letter picture card for the *m* upright in front of your child between two blocks or small boxes. Set up on a nearby chair or table the collection of toys you have assembled, whose names begin with the initial sounds [m], [l], and [f]. Ask your child to pick out only those toys which start with [m] and to place them in front of the letter picture card for the *m*.

It is entirely possible that your child has learned the alphabet names of the letters somewhere along the line, say from a television program. When he now sees the letter *m*, he'll call it *em*. You don't have to say "this is wrong." Just remind him to listen to the sound he hears. Your child will relearn rather quickly to give the sound name of the letter, and his knowledge of the alphabet name will fade into the background.

If your child was able to play this game of picking out the correct toys, you can now go on to the Letter-Writing Game.

II. Letter-Writing Game with One Letter

Prepare a sheet of paper on which you write the *m*s in dots. Draw an arrow to indicate where the child should start. Now explain: "If I say a word that starts with [m], you may trace a *m*. If I say another word, like Daddy or school, you must not move your pencil. Since these words do not start with [m], you cannot trace a *m*.

In all writing games I use lined commercial notebook paper (the largest width). In order to help children learn to

³ See Appendix I.

align their letters properly, I first prepare the page using three spaces defined by four lines. The two middle lines which are to contain the body, or core, of each letter are drawn with dark lines. The top line for the "up" letters and the bottom line for the "down" letters are drawn in lighter lines. Each horizontal "staff" of four lines is then separated by two spaces, so that it stands out clearly (see figure 8.2).

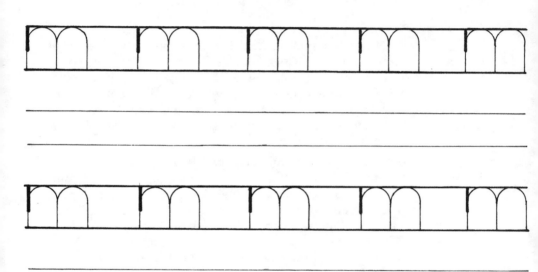

Figure 8.2.
Letter-writing game with one letter

It is important to the proper development of the readiness skills that your child not trace the *m*s without your supervision. Children who have very little spatial orientation or a marked tendency for reversals will not consistently trace the *m*s correctly. Long hard experience has proved that from the very first tracing of a letter, the child must learn to trace or write it correctly starting at the top and preceeding in the prescribed direction. In spite of the heavy starting line indicating which way the letters go, children who lack a directional sense frequently trace the letters incorrectly or backwards. *More harm is done if a child practices tracing the letter the wrong way than if he never practices it at all.*

III. The Folder Game with Initial Sounds

Paste two pockets side by side on a manila folder. Write m on one pocket and f on the other. Give a set of corresponding pictures to your child. As he turns up a picture, he has to put it in the correct pocket.

As your child learns more letters, use a folder with five handmade pockets. Write the letters to be mastered one on each pocket.

IV. The Mailman Game

Place the four letter picture cards between blocks so they are upright in front of your child. Have your collection of toys nearby. Your child can be the "mailman," to whom you might give a mailman's hat and bag to make the game more playful. Let the mailman select one object or toy and deliver it to the right address: the fork goes to the f, the mouse goes to the m. Any toys which begin with a different letter cannot be delivered at this time and are thus put on an empty chair, the "address unknown" place.

As a variation you can use pictures starting with these sounds and have your child deliver each picture to the proper address. Again include foils, i.e. pictures whose names start with sounds other than [m], [f], [l], or [a].

A harder variation is to play with plain printed letters instead of letter picture cards. Have the mailman deliver his mail to the plain letters. However, place the corresponding letter picture cards behind the child, so if he is uncertain about a given letter, he can turn around and check by finding its proper letter picture card.

V. Lotto Game with Pictures

For this game use 6 x 7½ white unlined cards as master cards. Rule each card so you have six squares. Draw the letter with its picture in the left space of the top row. Make one master card for each of the letters to be practiced, say m, f, l, and a.

Now from your collection select five small picture cards whose names start with [m], five whose names start with [f], and so on. Give two master cards to your child and two to yourself. Again the small cards are shuffled and placed in a pile in front of your child, who will be the caller. As he turns up a card, he will identify the picture, say its initial sound, and then you and he will check who can claim the card. For instance, the picture of a mirror would be claimed by the player who has the m-master card. The player who first fills all his master cards wins.

Most children also enjoy playing the lotto game as solitaire, sorting out all the small picture cards onto the proper master cards.

Later you can make this game more difficult by making new master cards and writing the actual letter in one of the squares of each master card, instead of a letter with its letter picture. The same small picture cards could be used with either variation of the sound lotto.

VI. Sorting Game with Envelopes

For this game take an ordinary manila folder and using masking tape make a pocket inside it. On the pocket, tape one of the big ms you've made. Take small envelopes and put a picture in each envelope. Use some pictures whose names start with [m] and some which do not.

Give the envelopes to your child. Ask him to open one envelope at a time. If the picture inside the envelope starts with [m], he can place the envelope in the pocket: if not he should discard it on a pile to the left of him.

When your child knows the letter m reasonably well and is eager to go ahead, introduce your letter picture for [f], following the same procedure as you did for the [m]. Ask your child to identify the picture of the fan and to give you its initial sound [f]. Always make sure that the child knows the meaning of each word studied. Trace the blue lines of the f with your finger, explaining that since this is a fan whose name starts with [f], the blue lines form the letter f.

From here on, go very slowly, depending on your child. Some children, like Bobby and Robin discussed earlier, find it very difficult to identify the m and the f without their letter pictures. If you feel that your child is not ready for more letters, you can play many of the following games with him.

Always place the letter pictures, in this case m and f, first in front, later in back of your child, so he can easily check for himself what the letters say whenever he needs to.

The letter pictures are a self-corrective tool, very much

like a dictionary. If your child has forgotten what a given letter says, he looks it up in the set of letter pictures. Once he has located the letter, he says out loud the name of the letter picture and listens to its first sound. He hears himself say the sound and thus, without your help, is able to deduce the sound name of the letter. He develops a sense of security knowing that he can look up a letter in case of uncertainty or to correct an error. He does not feel the burden of having to memorize a letter, nor is he subjected to the diminishing experience of being told that he is wrong or "You made a mistake."

VII. Making a Sound Book

For this activity manila paper or cheap drawing paper is required. Draw two lines at the bottom of the paper, and dot two rows of *m*s as you did in the Letter Writing Game. Be sure to make a heavy line indicating the starting point of each letter. Ask the child to tell you the sound name of the letter, then watch him trace the first letters. If he does not hesitate, then let him finish the job on his own. Provide him with some old magazines (mail-order catalogs are veritable gold mines) and some blunt kindergarten scissors. Suggest that he can make a Sound Book. Let him find pictures that start with [m], cut them out, and paste them on the *m*-page.

On a later day you can provide him with a *f*-page. Add pages to the Sound Book as your child learns new letters. After about five or six pages (many children want to do two or more pages for one letter) take a piece of colorful construction paper for a simple cover and staple it together with the pages he has completed. He has made his first book!

VIII. Filing Pictures Under Correct Letters

Children enjoy having a filing box. You can buy an inexpensive one that will hold 3 x 5 index cards, or with your child's help, you can make a filing box out of an old shoe box. Put tabs on top of some index cards which will then serve as dividers. On each tab write one of the letters which the child knows.

Give your child an old magazine or mail catalogs. On a plain index card write four letters, well spaced apart, which your child knows. He now must look for pictures whose names start with initial sounds corresponding to those letters. He cuts each picture out, pastes it on an index card, and then files it behind the proper letter.

IX. Grab Bag Game

Have your child close his eyes and pick one toy from a bag of toys. He is to say the name of the toy and then put it in front of the correct letter picture. Again, after a while, replace these letter pictures by index cards bearing the letters only.

As a variation you can have a prepared sheet with dotted *m*s and *f*s. If your child picks a toy whose name starts with [m], he can trace a *m*. If he picks one that starts with [f], he can trace a *f*. If he picks any other toy, he can identify its initial sound, but there is no corresponding letter to trace. To make the game more interesting you can each guess beforehand which line will win, the *m*s or the *f*s.

X. Fishing Game

Use metal toys starting with the initial sounds your child has learned. Write the initial letter for each toy on plain, unlined index cards and stand the cards on the couch. Put the toys in a box, and give your child a "rod" with a magnet attached to the line. Your child should "go fishing" without looking into the box. When he has caught a toy, he must tell you its initial sound and then place it in front of the correct letter.

This game requires some preparation and thought but is very well liked by many children and can be used again and again.

XI. Ball Pitching Game

Label three or four boxes with the latest letters your child has learned, using plain white paper labels and the letters without their letter pictures. Line the boxes in a row, and have your child stand at a designated place, about eight to ten feet away. Give him a ball or a beanbag. When you say a word, for instance, *a*pple, the child has to identify the initial sound orally and then throw the ball into the correct box, in this case the *a*-box.

XII. Hopscotch

Draw hopscotch games on the sidewalk or in the playground. Label each square with a letter your child knows. Your child throws a bean bag into the first square and says a word that starts with the corresponding sound. If he is right, he may hop through the squares. He can throw the beanbag again, this time to a different square, and again if he can think of an appropriate word, he may jump through all the squares.

These last three games are fun to play with a friend or friends provided they have been taught the sound names of the letters and not their alphabet names

XIII. Letter Writing Game with Two or More Letters

Prepare a red and blue lined sheet as you did in the previous Letter Writing Game. Now dot two lines of ms and two lines of fs. Indicate with heavy crayon where the letter should start. Explain to your child that if you say a word starting with [f], for instance, fork, he may trace a f. If you say a word starting with [m], he may trace a m. If you say a word starting with any other sound, he should not move his pencil. As your child advances and learns more letters, you can adapt this Letter Writing Game always using the last four letters studied.

Whenever your child needs practice in tracing a particular letter, use this or variations of this game rather than just letting him trace row after row of letters.

XIV. The Matching Game

Cut blank (unlined) 3 x 5 index cards in half. Write one m on each of five cards, and write one f on each of five cards. With your help have your child find and cut out five pictures starting with [m] and five pictures starting with [f]. Paste each picture on half an index card.

Now shuffle the letter and picture cards and place them face down in a deck between you. Take turns picking up one card. The picture cards should go to the right side of the table, the letter cards to the left. Say your child turns up the picture of a fork, if there is a f on the table, he can claim a trick. He takes both cards and places them together, face downward, close to him. Then it is your turn.

The player who can claim the most tricks wins.

As a variation show your child how to play a sorting game by himself; as he matches picture with corresponding letter, he turns the trick over. Many children enjoy playing this form of "solitaire" on a rainy day.

XV. The Snatching Game

Use the same deck of cards as you did in the Matching Game, only this time keep the letter and the picture cards in two separate piles. Put the letter cards face down in front of your child. Shuffle the picture cards and put them down in front of yourself. Now you both simultaneously turn up your top card and watch carefully for the two cards to match. The first one to see that a letter and a picture match yells out the sound name of the letter, snatches the other player's card, and claims the trick. The player who has the most cards wins.

As a variation the player can slap his fist on the table to indicate that a match exists and then identify the letter by its sound.

XVI. Letter Writing Game with the Stop-and-Go-Cube and Cards

For this game take a large die and cover two sides of it with red construction paper (or color them red with a magic marker). Cover the other sides with green paper (or color them green). Prepare a lined sheet as you did for previous Letter Writing Games; only this time prepare a second sheet for yourself or a visiting friend. Use the most recently learned letters, but not more than four at any one game.

From your collection of picture cards pick those that start with the sounds corresponding to the letters you are going to practice. Shuffle the cards and place them face down in front of the players. Now your child takes his turn throwing the die. If the green side is on top, it means "Go!" and he can turn up a card, say its name, and trace the corresponding letter on his sheet. Then it's your turn to throw the die. If it should land with the red side on top, it means "Stop!" and you lose your turn. The player who first finishes his sheet wins.

As a variation you can make a color wheel. Using heavy cardboard draw a circle on it and divide it into four sections. Color the sections alternately red and green. Make a hole in the middle and with a paper fastener attach a small disk with an arrow. The game is the same except that your child spins the arrow instead of throwing a die. If the arrow lands in the green section, it means "Go!" : your child can pick up a card and trace its corresponding letter. If it lands on red, it means "Stop!": the player loses his turn.

Games involving the tracing of letters are the single most effective activity in reinforcing the child's visual discrimination. Many children experience difficulty in *seeing* the difference between letters which to them appear quite similar; for instance, the m and the n look alike to many children. The kinesthetic experience of tracing these letters repeatedly makes them aware of the difference between these letters: they *feel* the letters and this feeling subsequently helps them to *see* them and thus be able to identify each one.

Almost all children commonly reverse the b and the d, the g and the p, since they "look alike" for a very long time. Even tracing activities often do not help here. If the child has forgotten the name or the shape of any of these letters, have him look it up and check it with the letter picture card. Don't ever supply the answer. If your child rechecks the name with its letter picture card, he is rewarded with the confidence that he can figure out on his own what each letter says.

In persistent cases of b- and d-reversal, a supplementary technique a parent can use is to draw a large clear b on a sheet of paper and hang it over the bed, desk, etc. for a time. The b should have a solid belly in front of it.

The child can draw or paste on pictures of objects starting with [b]. In a different room, say the kitchen, hang a piece of paper with the letter d, but alter its configuration slightly so that it is not solid. It is now completely differentiated from the b and also serves to remind the child of its letter picture, the duck.

Experience has taught me that many children take a disproportionately long time to learn the first four to six letters. As they get the hang of it, they learn each successive letter faster.

Let us suppose that your child has learned all of the letters. Where do you move now? By teaching him the digraphs *ch, th,* and *sh.* Again use letter pictures like *ch*ick, *th*ermometer, and *sh*ell to show him that the sound he hears at the beginning of each word is recorded by two letters which, when put together, form a new sound.

At this point your child can identify all lowercase letters. In school he will learn the capital form of the letters that he needs for reading and writing proper names and sentences. There is one exception. From the beginning teach him to write the first letter of his first name with a capital letter. This is the only capital letter you should teach your child.

Once your child knows all the letters, he may clamor to read words. At this point you may go ahead and set the stage for him to discover actual reading. The next chapter will show you how.

To those children who want to go on to actual reading, you must teach capital letters now, since capital letters are used at the beginning of proper names and sentences.

To help the child learn capital letters, print four capital letters at a time, using the sequence of letters as outlined in this chapter. Place these letters under the corresponding letter picture cards. Then play the letter writing games.

Special Help for Children with Difficulties

Many children have difficulties in developing a proper directional sense. Therefore they have a tendency to form letters by starting at the bottom instead of at the top, and by going from right to left. If your child has such difficulty, try the following games.

Using Raised Letters[4]

Let us suppose your child has trouble forming the *f* correctly. Have your child trace with his finger the *f* on its letter picture card several times. Be sure he starts at the top and goes from left to right when tracing the cross line. Place the letter picture for the *f* in front of the child. Give him these directions: "If I say a word that starts with [f], you may trace the raised letter. If I say a word that does *not* start with [f], you can't move your hand."

Making a Sound Book with Larger Letters

For a child with special learning difficulties, large size letters have proven to be helpful. We suggest you use the same size letters that you use in the letter picture cards, i.e. 1¼", 1¾", and 2" respectively.

As we have described before, to help your child make a sound book draw two lines on a blank page, 1¼" apart. Write the letter the child is practicing faintly in pencil. Emphasize the starting line with a heavy magic marker.

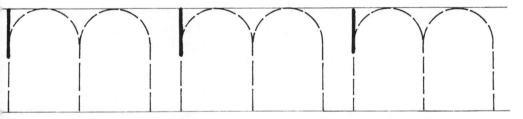

Figure 8.3.
Trace the letters. (This is the beginning of your child's sound book.)

Let your child trace each *m* with his finger. Make sure that he starts at the top and goes across from left to right on the cross line.

Variation of Letter Writing Game with Larger Letters

Put another sheet of two lines of *m*s in front of you. Say: "If I say a word that starts with [m], you can trace a *m*. If I say any other word, you can't move your pencil." If he makes a mistake, he must stop and give you a word that

---

[4] Raised letters may be purchased from: Touch Teaching Aids—Lower Case Letters, Childcraft Education Corporation, 20 Kilmer Road, Edison N.J. 08817

starts with [m]. The first player who traces all his ms wins. Let him win unobtrusively!

For variation use the Stop-and-Go Cube or a color wheel to give each of you a turn tracing letters.

Children who experience real difficulty in developing eye-hand coordination and a directional sense enjoy the last two variations of the Letter Writing Game so much that they never complain about the tracing activity, even though the task is extremely difficult for them.

Use of Letter Pictures as Aids in All Games

Some of my pupils feel so unsure about their ability to discriminate between two letters that they need the security of constantly being able to check the letter picture cards. Place the letter pictures of the letters your child is unsure about behind him so that at any time he can turn around and check what a particular letter says. If you have wall space, I suggest you tape the letter picture of the letter your child just learned on the wall.

Helping Children Write Their Name

Some children continue to write their names backward. Don't correct them. Unobtrusively dot the name on a piece of paper and mark clearly with a red crayon where the name starts. If you let this error slip by, it will be harder to break it later on. As a tracing game have him go over it the correct way.

Don't Increase Play Time

Don't increase the play time you spend with your child just because he has difficulties learning a letter. Be sure to stress the game aspect of the exercises so your child feels he is *playing* with you. Be patient. Any concern or pressure on your part defeats the real goal of helping your child gain a feeling of competence in an area where he has difficulties.

You have time. Once your child has mastered two letters, he has actually learned far more than just two letters: he has understood two facts: first, letters record sounds; and second, letters face a definite direction and have to be formed in a specific way. His understanding of the learning process that letters record sounds is the important result of your teaching, not the number of letters he knows. This insight is crucial for his success in learning to read.

Suppose your child has mastered only a few letters, say four to six, by the time he enters first grade, don't continue to teach him at home. At this point your teaching can actually interfere with his progress at school. The lines of authority must be clear. If they are not, your child will become confused and may conclude that you have no faith in his teacher. Obviously, an occasional game does no harm. Of course, it is also important that you express interest in your child's work and help him to develop good work habits by setting aside a definite time and a quiet place where he can do his homework. Your pride and excitement in his intellectual progress are very important to him, spurring him on to do more.

Stop If These Suggestions Do Not Work

Stop playing these games if you find yourself saying to your child "that is wrong" or if your child balks at playing even the simplest games outlined above. Do not go on, but don't give up. At this point play it safe and get an evaluation of your child's learning difficulties from a psychologist or pediatrician to determine if your child has specific learning disabilities. Be sure to consult a professional who is convinced of the necessity of early intervention, not one who says: "Don't worry; he'll outgrow these problems in time."

There is no cause to be alarmed. Children with even severe learning disabilities do learn to read, but they cannot be taught by their parents. In chapters ten and eleven you will find suggestions on who can teach your child.

Sequence of Letters and Suggested Pictures for Each Letter

[m]
magnet, mirror, marble, milk bottle, mop, mailbox, monkey, mouse, mitten, magazine, matches, mask

[f]
feather, fern, fork, football, fan, fish, fishing rod

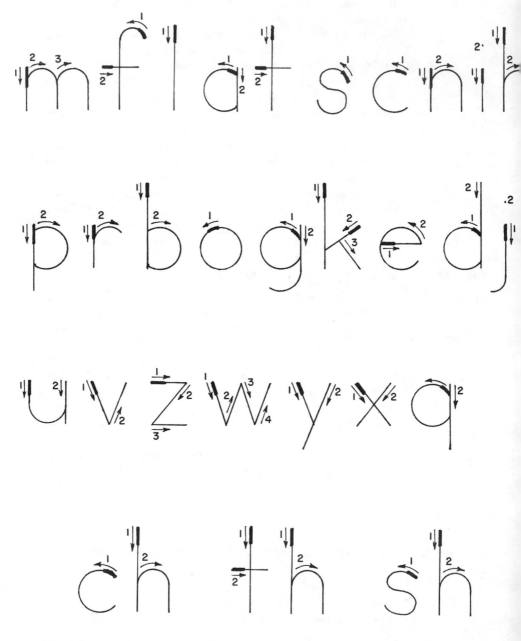

Figure 8.4.
The lowercase letters, indicating the sequential movement of pencil strokes

[l]
lemon, lion, lamb, ladder, lipstick, loaf, lid, letter, lock, lime, leaf, lollipop, lamp, leopard, lettuce

[ă]
ax, anchor, ant, apple, ambulance, astronaut

[t]
telephone, towel, toothbrush, tie, tent, tomato, turtle, teapot, top, tiger, toothpaste, table, turkey

[s]
sandwich, saw, sailboat, soap, salt, seal, sock

initial [k] spelled c
cup, cap, candle, curtain, cabbage, carrot, cake, camel, cat, cane, can, cape, cookie, candy, corn, comb

[n]
nest, net, needle, napkin, nut, nail, nurse, numerals, newspaper, necktie, note, nickel

[i]
igloo, inch, indian, ink, insect

[h]
hat, hose, hammer, hen, hanger, heart, house, horse, horn, handbag, hatchet, helicopter, hand, hoe

[p]
paper, perfume, pizza, penny, pin, pail, peacock, pie, puppet, pipe, pelican, paintbrush

[r]
raccoon, raisin, ribbon, radio, rope, rake, radish, robot, rocket, rose, rooster, ring

[b]
beads, bicycle, box, belt, bat, boot, ball, bell, balloon, book, buckle, bee, bib, basket, bull, bowl.

[o]
olive, ostrich, otter, ox, orchid, octopus, orange

[g]
gum, garage, golf club, guitar, goose, gift

initial [k] spelled k

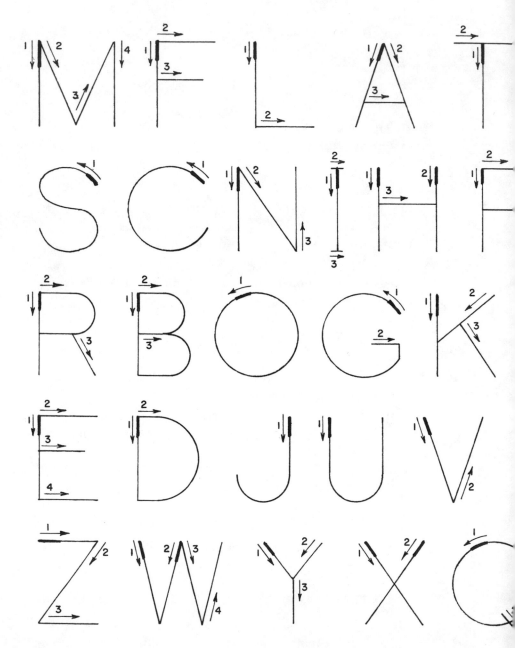

Figure 8.5.
The capital letters, indicating the sequential movement of pencil strokes

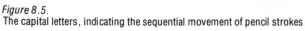

kangaroo, key, kerchief, king, kite, kettle, kitten

[e]
egg, elephant, elf, envelope, Eskimo

[d]
doctor, dish, daisy, duck, doughnut, dime, domino

[j]
jacket, jump rope, jacks, jam, jar

[u]
umpire, umbrella, Uncle Sam

[v]
vinegar, vase, violin, violet, vest, valentine

[z]
zebra, zoo, zinnia, zero, zipper

[w]
wagon, wigwam, windmill, watermelon, wallet, wishbone, web, witch

[y]
yo-yo, yak, yarn, yardstick, yolk

[q]
quail, quilt, queen, question mark, quarter (coin), quotes

[ch]
church, chick, chocolate, chimney, cherries, chipmunk, chain, cheese, checkers

[th]
thistle, thermometer, thimble, thorn

[sh]
sheep, shovel, ship, shoe, shell, shirt

SETTING THE STAGE FOR READING

The step from mere sound-letter matching to actual reading presents a new phase in the reading process and one that needs your guidance. Many children who proceed to put letters together on their own can get into trouble. They may start out by sounding out words letter by letter: [m] [a] [n]. Although they can put sounds together, they do not really understand the meaning of the word.

One of the signs that your child is ready to go on to actual reading is when he begins to sound out words whenever he can. Another is when he begins writing words by putting letters together. These are signals that he is ready for the games described in this chapter.

In the beginning, introduce him only to the reading vocabulary specified in this chapter. Don't teach your child to read from books which contain words that are spelled irregularly, no matter how easy and attractive they look to you. Use only the games listed in this chapter at this stage. To present him with such linguistically irregular words as *say, hall, far, tall,* and *said,* where every word contains the letter *a* but each time with a different sound, makes it extremely difficult for your child to figure out on his own a new word containing the letter *a.* Stick with regularly spelled words like *cap, hat, pan,* or *bag,* where the *ă* has the same sound each time. Once your child has decoded a few of these words in play sessions, he will discover that he can read words on his own! Children themselves are quick to realize their newly won decoding power as the following comments show.

Robin (5:4) read by transfer a new word: "Ra-n? Ran! Oh, he *ran* away. I never did that before. I read it! I read it!"

Bruce (5:9) had just read five short-a words on his own. He was breathless with excitement. "This is a lot better than reading fake words like I do at home." Questioned as to what he meant by fake words, Bruce explained that his mother would show him words in the book she was reading aloud to him and he would "read" the words back to her.

Preparation for Word Games

For the next activities and games collect a great many pictures from magazines, catalogs, or inexpensive picture dictionaries.[1] The picture should be no larger than 2½″ x 3″ (one-half of a standard 3 x 5 index card). Suggested words are:

hat	pad	gas
man	pan	cab
cap	can	nap
cat	ham	dad
fan	map	rag
bat	bag	sat
mat	jam	ran

It is advisable to have at least four or five clearly identifiable pictures for every one of these words, so you can make several games. You may find it simpler to draw or trace them than to cut them out. You can use the same picture five times, e.g. have five identical pictures of a cat. The games that follow introduce your child to his first reading of words.[2]

I. Riddle Game Introducing Short-[ă] Words

preparation: As always, start with the spoken language. Guide your child into the next phase of learning, which is the analysis of spoken words. Instead of concentrating on initial sounds, show him how to break the spoken word into main parts and its ending, e.g. [ma] - [n]. Paste six pictures of objects or animals whose names are short-[ă] words on 3 × 5 blank index cards. Use suggested pictures listed above. Stand them up before the child.

how to play: Now pronounce the name of a picture in two distinct parts (e.g. ha - t) and ask him to indicate which one it is. If he points to the correct picture, he can take it as a trick. On another day play the game so the two of you take turns asking for pictures in the same way. Continue with this game until your child is used to this new procedure.

[1] See appendix for commercially available materials.

[2] Much of this material is covered at great length in the Teachers Guide to Book B, *We Discover Reading*, Structural Reading Program, New York: Random House, 1972.

II. Word Cards with Word Dominoes

preparation: For this game you need to make a *new* set of cards which will have pictures representing short-[ă] words and the corresponding words underneath them. Paste one picture on a card, e.g. the picture of a man, and then write the word *man* underneath, leaving a gap between the main part of the word *ma* and its ending *n*. Print the consonants in blue and the vowels in red (see figure 9.1).

Construct your own word dominoes by cutting blank 3 × 5 index cards into eight equal parts of 1¼" × 1½". Print the main-parts of the short-[ă] words on one set of word dominoes. Again write the consonants in blue and the vowels in red (see figure 9.2).

how to play: Place the set of word cards face down in a pile. Ask your child to pick up the first card, e.g. the picture of a *cat*. Explain that in all of these reading games, in case of disagreement, he has to accept your definition of a picture since each of the pictures stands for a specific spoken word; e.g. he must accept that it is the picture of a *cat*, not a *kitten*.

Have your child repeat the name of the picture on his card, [cat]. Now invite him to read the word underneath. He'll probably read it in two parts ca-t. Immediately afterward have him read the word again and tell you what the word means: this time he'll read the word fluently, in one piece ("Cat! It's an animal that meows. I wish we had a cat"). In this way your child has put the word he has read back into the spoken language, proving that he has understood its meaning. Thus he comes to realize that reading means two things: decoding a word accurately and comprehending its meaning.

When he has read all the cards, use the word dominoes. Place the word dominoes with the main word parts (such as *ca*, *ma*, *ha*, *fa*) face down above the spread-out picture cards. Put the word dominoes bearing the word endings

[3] The gap between main part and ending helps your child to more easily decode. Also the color coding is helpful because it accentuates the chief characteristic of each word, i.e. its vowel. However, it's not necessary to explain the terms vowel and consonant to your child at this point.

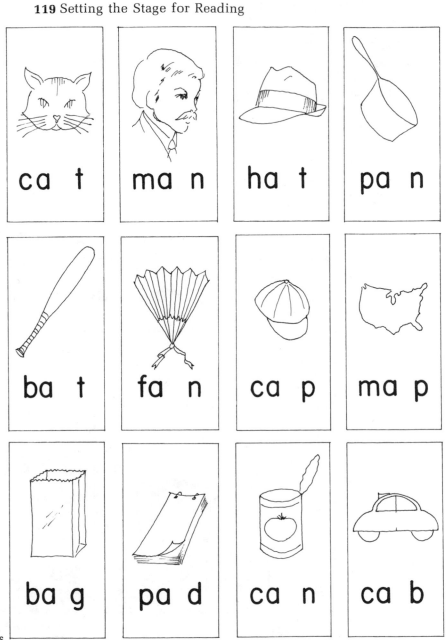

Figure 9.1.
Word cards

face up to the right side of the picture cards (see figure 9.3).

As the child turns up a main-part domino, he reads it in one flow; e.g. he says [ma], and then finds the card where

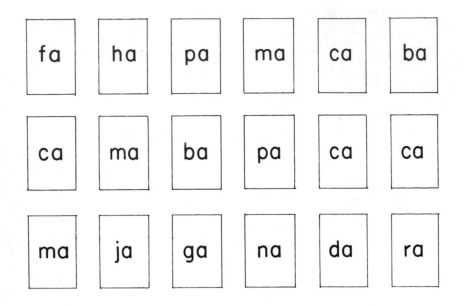

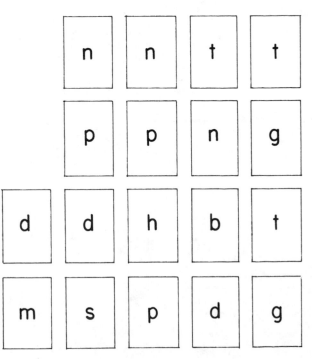

Figure 9.2.
Word dominoes

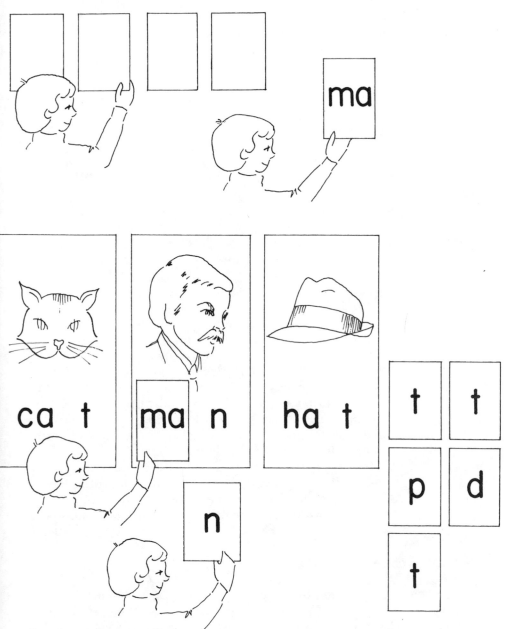

Figure 9.3.
Using word cards with word dominoes

it belongs, in this case the picture of a man. He places the domino *ma* on top of the picture, and scanning the word ending dominoes, picks out the appropriate one to complete the word *man*. Have your child build all of the words on the cards.

Building words with the word dominoes is also a good preparation for spelling. It helps your child to practice the "thinking" part of spelling without the added task of writing the letters.

For the next few days play this game only adding three new word cards (or more if your child wants to) each day until your child can read about twenty words. Then he is ready for the next games.

III. Domino and Folder Game

preparation: On each inner side of a manila folder paste six pictures of short-[ă] words which you prepared at the start of this chapter. Sitting next to your child, lay the folder on the table between you. The side of the folder in front of the child is his side to play on, the other is yours. Now place the main word part dominoes face down along the top of the folder. Divide the word endings between you and place them to each side of the folder.

how to play: After your child has identified each picture in the folder, he picks up a main-part domino, reads it as a whole, and then sees if he has a picture it would fit. For instance, he turns up the *ca*; if he has the picture of a cap, he puts the domino on the picture. He should then say *cap* to himself and hunt for the *p* among the endings.

After all the words have been built (covering up the pictures), call for a domino-word by a simple definition or riddle (e.g. "what goes on your head?"). Your child has to scan all the words he has built to find the one you asked for.

IV. Picture Lotto with Word Dominoes

preparation: Cut two master cards, 6 × 7½, from oaktag or cardboard. Draw six equal squares in pencil on each card. Paste one of the short-[ă] pictures you prepared at the beginning of the chapter on each square (see figure 9.4).

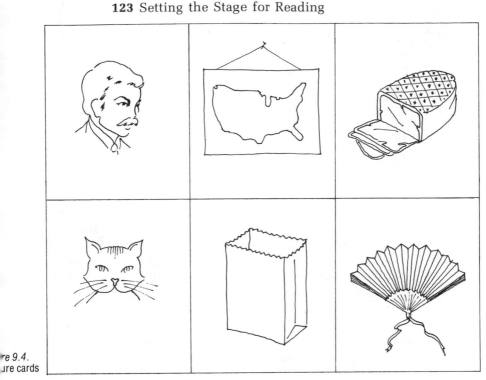

Figure 9.4.
Picture cards

how to play: Give your child one master card to put before him, and place the other one in front of you. Put the main word parts of the dominoes face down in front of the cards. Line up the endings, face up, to the sides.

Your child is the caller. He turns up a main-word part and names it. Then comes the excitement: which of the two players can first claim it as his card? Whoever has claimed the main-word part now looks for the proper ending to complete the word. The player who has first built all the words on his master card wins.

Many children enjoy playing lotto as solitaire. In this case give your child both master cards, place the word dominoes in position, and let him build the words for the pictures on both cards.

Your child is now ready for his first writing games. Writing words naturally reinforces reading. It makes sense to the child that he learns spelling as the natural counterpart to reading. Furthermore, he wants to put into writing what he wants to say, and he is keenly aware that spelling, like reading, means figuring out. When Lisa had to record the word *nap* she turned to me: "I always think before I write it," and then proceeded to say the word [nap] to herself recording each sound as she heard it.

Lisa (6:3) writes *tug* on her own. She looks at the word and bursts out: "I know how to spell. I know how to spell."

The same child wrote five words on her own in her worktext, commenting, "It was magic. I wrote all the words, and I didn't have any words to look at."

V. Picture Cards and Writing Words

preparation: For this game you make a new set of ten picture cards representing short-[ă] words. This time you don't write complete words underneath the pictures. Instead, write only the main part of each word on lines you have drawn before (see figure 9.5).

how to play: Place the picture cards face down in front of your child. As he turns up each card, have him name its picture, read the main word part underneath *(ma)*, and say the name of the picture again, this time emphasizing its ending, man. He should then complete the word underneath the picture by recording the [n] he hears. Finally have him read the whole word back to you before he goes on to the next cards.

Your child will very soon ask to write entire words on his own. At this point I would let him choose a colored folder at the stationery store and insert blank—not lined—white pages and write his name on his first Writing Book. Let him illustrate the cover if he wishes. Each time he has finished a writing game, let him put the sheet in his folder.

VI. Writing Game with Toys

preparation: Draw sets of four lines leaving ample space between the sets.

Collect in a large paper bag toys or objects whose names represent short-[ă] words, e.g. a fan, pad, bag, hat, cap, (toy) cat, map, man, can, jam, bat, rag, bag.

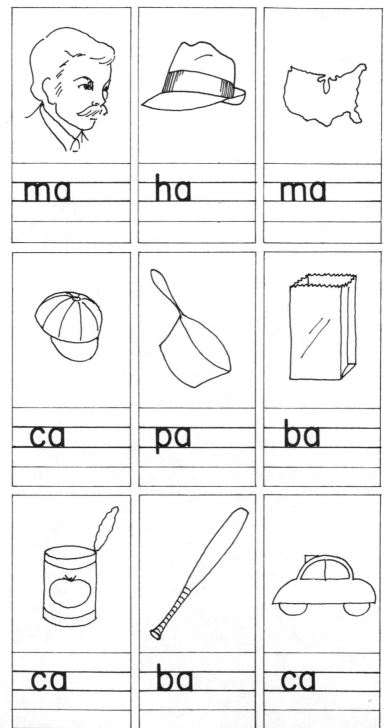

Figure 9.5.
Picture cards
with word parts

how to play: Give your child the prepared sheet of paper. Have him shut his eyes and touch a toy from the bag. Let him guess what it is, and then, eyes open, take the toy out and check if he is right. Then ask him to record its name on his sheet of paper.

As a preliminary step he can build each word with the word dominoes first if he wants to. Set up the word dominoes as usual, the main word parts face up above the picture cards, the endings to the side.

VII. Writing Game with the Stop-and-Go-Cube

preparation: Use the Stop-and-Go-Cube as described in chapter eight. Have the bag of toys and the word dominoes ready. Give your child a prepared sheet, and put a piece of lined notebook paper in front of you.

how to play: Your child rolls the die. If it lands on green he may, with closed eyes, pick out a toy from the bag. Now have him write its name on his sheet of paper. If the die lands on red, he loses his turn. Now it's your turn. Roll the die. If it lands on green, you pick out a toy and record its name. The player who has first written five words has won.

As before, if your child wants to, let him first build each word with the dominoes and then write it.

VIII. Write Down What Is Missing

preparation: Give your child a prepared sheet with sets of four lines. Have ready a tray and toys or objects representing short-[ă] words.

how to play: Put five of the objects on the tray. After your child has looked at everything on the tray, have him close his eyes. Take one object away. He can now open his eyes, figure out what you removed, and write down what is missing. He'll read it to you so you can both check if he is right.

After a while he'll want to take a toy away for you and have you write down what is missing. Be sure to write the words in manuscript, using red for vowels and blue for consonants, so your child can easily check your paper.

IX. Riddle Game and Writing Words

preparation: Line a piece of paper as before.

how to play: Give the paper to your child. Make up a simple riddle whose answer is a short-[ă] word. For example, "You need this to find your way in a strange city" (map). Have him guess the riddle and then record the word.

If he insists on giving you a riddle, place before him a set of pictures representing short-[ă] words and say that both your riddle and his have to refer to one of these pictures.

X. What Is My Name?

preparation: On a blank notebook size paper mark six squares in rows of two each. You or your child paste six pictures representing short-[ă] words, one in each square. Draw four lines under each picture. Have the Stop-and-Go-Cube ready, and make a similar page for yourself.

how to play: Your child throws the die. If it turns up green, he can write the name for the first picture on his page. If it turns up red, it is your turn to label a picture. The player who first labels all his pictures wins.

Many children enjoy labeling the pictures on their own without playing a game. They may even ask for more pages to do.

As a variation of the above, leave out the pictures and instead write six words very faintly under each of the blank spaces. Have your child read each word, go over it with a pencil, and then draw on his own a picture in the blank above the word. The drawing accomplished is to be recommended and not corrected.

XI. Find the Word

preparation: Have ready a deck of picture cards representing short-[ă] words. With faint pencil lines print half of the list of these words on a piece of paper that you have lined for your child. Write the remaining on another piece of paper for yourself.

how to play: Shuffle the cards and place them face down in a pile between you and your child. As he picks up a card, he reads the word and then scans the words on his sheet. If the word is on his sheet, he traces over it with his pencil. If it is not, he puts the picture card in a discard pile. Now it's your turn. The game has ended when there are no more picture cards. The player who has written the most words wins.

This is another good game played as solitaire. Print the words on a piece of paper in light lines, and give your child the corresponding picture cards. As he turns up each picture, he'll find the word on his paper and trace it. The game is finished when your child has written all the words.

This is an excellent game, for it provides not only practice in tracing (which some children need as a reinforcement for those letters that they may not be sure of), but it gives practice in reading. The child is actually scanning a list of words until he finds the right one.

If in any of the games your child has misspelled a word, don't correct him. Encourage him to read the word back to himself. He can correct his spelling error by proofreading the word, again and again if necessary. In this way the child develops independent skill and increases his confidence in his own spelling ability.

The next group of games, all card games, are designed to help your child proceed from the careful decoding of words to the reading of them fluently. Eventually he'll be able to merely glance at a word and grasp its meaning.

As a general preparation for the card games cut 3 × 5 index cards in half. Paste one picture representing a short-[ă] word on half of a card, e.g. the picture of a bag. On the other half write the corresponding word, in this case *bag*. At this point write the word *bag* as a whole unit without leaving a gap between the main part and ending. Print the consonants in blue and the vowels in red.

XII. The Matching Game

preparation: From your collection choose fourteen picture cards representing short-[ă] words and their corresponding word cards.

how to play: Shuffle the cards and place in a pile face down in front of you. Your child turns up the first card, e.g. the picture of a *man,* and puts it in front of him. Your turn is next. Pick up a card; suppose it's a card with the word *cat* written on it. If your child now turns up the card with the picture of a cat, he can match your word card and, putting the cards together, has taken his first trick. If he should turn up the card with the word *hat,* he'd match his own picture card of a hat, and also have a trick.

Continue taking turns until there are no more cards. The player who has the most tricks wins.

This game can also be played alone. You shuffle the cards and place them face down in front of him. As the child turns up a picture card, he puts it to the left of him. As he turns up a word card, he places it to the right. Whenever he sees two cards that match, he pairs them as a trick, continuing until he has matched up all the cards.

XIII. The Snatching Game

Use the same deck of cards containing picture and matching word cards.

how to play: Place the word cards face down in front of your child. Shuffle the picture cards and put them face down in front of you. Now you both simultaneously turn up your top card watching carefully if the two cards match. The first one to see that a word and a picture match yells out the word, snatches the other player's card, and claims the trick. The player who has the most cards wins.

XIV. Word Lotto

preparation: Use eighteen 3 × 5 blank index cards. They will be the master cards. Draw a vertical line down the middle. Write on the left side of each card a short-[ă] word in red for vowels and blue for consonants. The right side stays blank. It will be covered with the corresponding picture.

Now cut nine index cards in half. Paste a picture corresponding to each of the eighteen words, and on the reverse side write the word that names it.

how to play: Each player has nine master cards spread out in front of him. Now place the word cards between you: the words face up. Your child reads aloud the word, e.g. *cat,* and then turns the card over to look at the picture and check that he has read the word correctly. Whoever has the master card with the word *cat* claims the picture and puts it on the blank space of this card. The first player to fill all his master cards wins.

As your child looks to see if he has the particular master card needed, he has to scan all his cards. This develops his ability to read the words fluently, at sight.

This game can also be played alone.

XV. Winning with Tricks

preparation: Use twelve short-[ă] word cards and their corresponding pictures, which you have prepared earlier.

how to play: Shuffle the word cards and put them face down in a pile. Deal the picture cards alternately to your child and yourself and hold them in your hands. Now let your child turn up a word card from the pile and read it. If he has the corresponding picture card in his hand, he puts it down in the middle of the table together with its word card as his trick. Now it's your turn. Pick up a word card and see if you make a trick. The player who has discarded all of his picture cards first and thus has the most tricks wins the game. This game, too, is popular as solitaire.

XVI. Slapjack

preparation: This is a rhyming game. Suggested rhyming sets are: man-can; hat-cat; nap-lap; bag-rag; ran-fan; sat-bat; pad-sad; map-cap.

Cut eight 3 × 5 index cards in half. Take two halves and write a rhyming set on each half. Continue until you have used up all eight rhyming sets. Remember to write the consonants in blue and the vowels in red.

how to play: Shuffle the cards and divide them, face down, between you and your child. Each player turns over a card at the same time and places it next to the other player's. If the words on these cards do not rhyme, each player takes another card. When the words do rhyme, both players slap their hands on the cards. The player who slaps his hand first takes the other player's pile of discards and adds it to his own stock pile. The game ends when one player has captured all the other's cards.

As you go on with these games, your child will probably develop a favorite that he'll want to play each day. That's fine. This repertoire is given simply to provide you with variety.

Teaching the Short-[ĭ] words

If your child has enjoyed learning to read the short-[ă] words and urges you to teach him more, then it's time to introduce him to the short-[ĭ] words. Since your child now understands how to proceed from the spoken to the written short-[ă] word, it will take far less time and effort for him to read the short-[ĭ] words. Such progress comes about when a child is taught through understanding rather than by rote. He is able to apply previous knowledge to new tasks, a process which is called transfer, and which is imminently satisfying to the child. He will realize himself how many words he can discover on his own, and a sense of achievement will give additional momentum to his eagerness in learning to read.

Preparation for Word Games

Prepare new pictures for teaching the short-[ĭ] words. Suggested words are:

pin	dish	mix
lid	mill	fix
six	hill	hit
kit	lip	dig
pig	pill	wig
ship	fish	dip
bib	sit	zip

Use the same game in sequence with the short-[ĭ] words as you did with the short-[ă] words.

Once your child knows the short-[ă] and the short-[ĭ] words, you can introduce him to these new games.

XVII. The Sorting Game

preparation: Take a sheet of notebook paper and draw a column on it, each one headed by a key word, such as *man* and *bib*.

how to play: Now give a simple riddle, for instance "It is an animal that meows." Your child solves the riddle and then writes the word in the proper column.

As a variation take a second sheet of paper for yourself. Draw a column. Choose eight of the picture cards representing short-[ă] words and eight of the picture cards representing short-[ĭ] words. Add four cards each bearing a big red Stop sign. Shuffle all the cards and place them face down in front of you. Take turns picking up a picture card and writing the corresponding word in its proper column. Of course, if one of you draws a Stop card, you lose a turn. The player who has written the most words wins the game.

XVIII. The Filing Box

preparation: Buy an inexpensive filing box for 3 × 5 index cards. Either buy two dividers that have tabs on them or make your own by pasting gummed labels on index cards. Write *hat* on the tab of one divider and the word *six* on another. Be sure your child can readily see the tabs. Again choose eight picture cards representing short-[ă] words and eight picture cards representing short-[ĭ] words.

how to play: Shuffle the cards and then place the deck face down in front of your child. He picks up a card, says the name of the picture, and then writes it on a blank index card. Encourage him to illustrate it simply (or he can cut out a picture from a magazine or mail-order catalog and paste it above the word), and have him file the card behind its proper key word.

When your child has filed all the cards, you can use the following variation. Ask him to take out all of his filing cards. Shuffle them and place them face downward in front of him. When you say "Go!" he must turn up one card after another as fast as he can, read it, and file it behind its proper key word. When he has filed away all his cards he says "Stop!" Check how long it took him to file his cards. Write down the time it took on a pad as his score. He'll want to play the game again to improve his score. Not only does he have fun competing against himself but, at the same time, he gains speed in reading these words fluently.

As other vowel groups are introduced, write its key word, e.g. *log*, on the tab. Your child now adds the short-[ŏ] words to his filing box.

Once your child can read the short-[ă] and the short-[ĭ] words fluently, you can introduce him to very simple sentences. Sentence reading, analogous to learning to talk in simple sentences, is a decidedly more complex process than reading single words. The child has to figure out the relationship of the words to each other in order to extract the meaning from the sentence as a whole. The first sentences your child reads are very simple.

Introducing Sentences on the Spoken Level

Teach your child on the spoken level the difference between an incomplete sentence, such as *my blue sweater*, and a complete sentence, such as *Anne has a blue sweater*. Explain that in writing we put a dot, called a period, after a complete sentence, and we start the first word of the next sentence with a capital letter. Don't dwell on this. Your child does not need to remember the term *period* or even understand the concept of what constitutes a complete sentence. He will learn these in first grade. You are merely preparing him for this later learning.

To read simple sentences your child needs to read the words *has* and *is*. Always introduce new words in a spoken sentence. Hence use the words *has* and *is* in sentences and then write these words down using blue for the consonants and red for the vowels. Have your child read each word and use it in a sentence.

Introduce the article *a* in an oral sentence, e.g. say "Mom has *a* pencil." Then write the article *a* down in black. Your child will realize that it looks like the short vowel *a*. Explain that since the *a* sounds slightly different from the pure vowel sound heard in *man* or *can*, you print it in black. You are going to write all irregular words in black.

Follow the same procedure with the article *the*. Use the word in a sentence and then write it down in black. Your child knows the *th* from the letter picture cards. Explain that the sound heard at the end of *the* is recorded by *e*.

XIX. The Nonsense Game

preparation: Cut 5 × 8 inch index cards into one third and two thirds each. Write the following nouns one each on the smaller size cards, and the predicates one each on the larger size.

Dad	has ham.
Sam	has a fish.
Ann	has a pad.
The cat	has a bat.
The fish	has a cap.
The hill	is in the pan.
The pig	has a bib.
Jill	is in the can.

Shuffle the subjects and place them face downward in one pile. Do the same for the predicates.

how to play: Your child picks up first a subject and then a predicate. He reads the sentences and decides if the sentence makes sense or if it is nonsense. If it is nonsense, he can keep the cards as a trick. Then it's your turn. Again only if the sentence makes no sense can you keep the two cards, subject and predicate, as a trick. The player who has the most tricks has won.

XX. Making a Nonsense Book

Put several blank notebook pages in a folder. Let your child decorate it. Write as its title: *My Nonsense Book.* Let your child trace the title and let him add his name.

Now write one simple sentence at the bottom of each page. Let your child illustrate it.

If your child wants to go on, teach him the short-[ŏ], then the short-[ŭ] and finally the short-[ĕ] words. The vocabulary for each new group is listed below:

short-o [ŏ] words:

mop	top	dog
pot	cot	log
fox	box	rod
pot	log	hop
doll	dot	cot
ox		

short-u [ŭ] words:

mud	run	tub
nut	hut	cup
rug	gum	jug
tug	sun	bud
bus	bug	bun
cut		

short-e [ĕ] words:

bed	leg	wet
ten	egg	pen
hen	peg	red
well	men	net
set	pet	bell
get		

Each time prepare a set of new pictures before you start teaching. Use the same games in sequence as you did with the short-[ă] words.

As your child's reading vocabulary expands, *The Sorting Game, The Filing Box, The Nonsense Game,* and *The Nonsense Book* will, of course, become more interesting.

At this point your child can read, write, and spell about ninety words, and he can read simple sentences containing linguistically regular words. This is a solid foundation on which your child's future reading skill will develop. More important than the number of words is your child's awareness that real reading means accurate decoding and the comprehension of a particular word. He has begun to understand the learning-to-read process. This is far more important than the number of words or the content of what he can read.

This is a good point at which to stop, especially if your child is going to first grade.[4] You have started your child on learning to read through understanding the structure of

[4] If your child is not yet going to first grade and pressures you to teach him more, then let him go through Book B, *We Discover Reading* and Book C, *We Read and Write,* of the Structural Reading Program (see reference 1 of Appendix). After these worktexts your child will read any book at first or even second grade level.

each word. His confidence that he can read words on his own is as important a stepping stone to reading as the actual decoding skill.

In my own practice I have found that at this point my preschool pupils have a keen understanding of what learning to read means. At times they may impatiently guess at a word by looking at the picture. But when I quietly point to the word itself, they are thrilled to find out that they actually have the reading power to correct their errors. That this insight occurs even at this beginning stage is shown by the following excerpts of my pupils' records. I recall vividly how excited Robin, Lisa, and Bobby became when they were really reading on their own without my help.

Robin (5:3) was working in Book B. Impatiently she looked at a picture and then guessed: "Chocolate sundae." Quietly I pointed to the printed word underneath the picture. This time Robin decoded the word: "ja-m. jam!" Then she commented, "I didn't read it at first. I just guessed, but I have to read. If I guess, I won't know how to read." A week later Robin guessed from a picture that the word said *man*. When I pointed to the word underneath the picture, Robin read the word carefully: "da-d, dad! I thought it was a man from the picture, but it says Dad, so they mean Dad . . . I can read words. This is real reading!"

Lisa (6:1) was also working in Book B. At one point she took a quick guess at a picture and said, "rug." I pointed my pencil to the printed word underneath and Lisa read: "ma-t, mat!" Then she added, "Toni, the picture looks like a rug but the word doesn't. I have to read the word."

Bobby (5:9) was working in Book B and guessed from a picture that the word said "tank." When I pointed to the word underneath the picture he corrected himself: "ga-s. gas! The word says gas. Now that is reading."
Six months later Bobby turned to another page in Book B while studying on his own. As he attempted to figure

out the first line, he commented, "You cannot always tell from the picture. You really can't. But you can always tell from the writing. You can figure out what it says."

10

ALTERNATIVES TO PARENT TEACHING

We have all heard humorous stories of what happens when a husband sets out to teach his wife to drive. And, looking at their own experience, many readers will ask, should members of a family who are emotionally close try to teach each other any kind of skill? It is true that in such instances, the pupil is often vulnerable and easily feels put down. Very often the teaching situation in itself is taken as implied criticism.

With the preschool child the situation is likely to be easier. In the first place, he enjoys the undivided attention, perhaps in a family where it is not always easy to come by. Secondly, although the child is learning, what he relishes is the fact that you are playing games together. Because the materials used allow him to correct his own mistakes, you are never forced into the pedagogical position of saying: "You are wrong." This automatically reduces the strains of a teacher/pupil relationship.

Parents who have enjoyed playing simple games with their children will find that teaching reading readiness is much the same and equally enjoyable. What it takes is patience, a relaxed view of the immediate goals to be achieved, and above all a sense of shared fun.

Fathers are sometimes more effective teachers than mothers simply because their patience is less eroded by exposure. They enjoy seeing their children learn, and many of them welcome a concrete plan of action such as a session of readiness games as a pleasant way of spending time with them. If, however, you are not a patient person, if your expectations are too high and you worry when your child takes too long to catch on, you may not be able to teach him. Your impatience communicates itself and only defeats its purpose.

As always, there are no hard and fast rules here, and it is difficult to assess when parents should definitely stay out of this whole area. In general, the achievement-oriented person with a strong educational mission is not likely to be a successful teacher. He expects results too quickly at a time when the child should be allowed to set his own pace. He is also likely to persist after the child has lost interest. Rigidity of any kind, either by insisting on certain games or on a definite time schedule, can have unhappy and often lasting results in terms of a child's spontaneous pleasure in learning.

If for some reason you cannot give your undivided attention to your child in these readiness sessions, it is probably better not to attempt it at all. Children are quick to sense when an adult's attention is elsewhere, and this can cause real resistance. If you really want to teach your child, and distractions from younger members of the family are too great, hire a baby sitter for an hour and set that time aside for yourself and your pupil.

There are families where there is an obvious clash of temperaments between parent and child—sometimes because they are so similar. If this is true of you and your child, you should not teach him. The chances are you will never be comfortable together in a games situation.

But don't think that difficulties in a teaching situation are always due to the parent. There are children who, for any number of reasons, feel compelled to fight their parents every step of the way. Without guilt or defeatism, we must accept the fact that our children, like everyone else, are different: some seem to have more "difficult" temperaments than others and are harder to raise. Second or third children often seem easier to bring up simply because we are more experienced, and therefore, more relaxed as parents.

If your child is a fighter, asserting himself stubbornly and negatively at any suggestion from you, however subtly made, you may have difficulty even getting him to listen to a story or to play readiness games. Rather than letting conflicts occur, stop immediately and bow out gracefully. Even if you have to let the teaching go for months, or finally find a good substitute, never risk a confrontation, because you will never win—simply because you are his parent. It is possible that his resistance toward the games, for instance, is really directed at your authority. By forcing your child to learn, you're taking the chance that he will transfer his negativism from you to the act of reading. Once he is against reading, that negativism is very difficult to change.

There are families, however, in which purposeful games can provide a rebellious youngster with a successful new medium of exchange with his parent that transcends the old pattern. Suppose, for example, that a three-and-a-half-to four-year-old is jealous of a new baby in the home and shows his anger by saying "no" to everything. What the child really wants is more of his mother's undivided attention. By playing readiness games with her troublesome child and reading to him, the mother could give him a sense of an enjoyable new status.

It is not always a new baby who arouses jealousy; it may well be a younger sibling who, because of his age, requires more help and attention from the parent and thus makes the older child feel angry and rejected. Having a special time with the parent and playing reading readiness games, which, after all, are "too difficult" for the younger brother or sister can convince the older child that there are a great many advantages to being older.

A word should be said about the child who at first has enjoyed playing games with a parent but who subsequently finds the tasks too difficult. If your child says: "It's too hard. I don't want to," slow down, backtrack, or even temporarily stop. Sometimes a parent's anxiety that his child is not learning may prevent him from helping the child over the next hurdle without seeming to push. Nor will the child respond as well to a parent's encouragement as he might to a stranger's.

You should not teach your own child if he has even just a few of the learning disabilities similar to the ones described in this book. None of the children whose records you read here could have been taught by their parents. In each case, there were different reasons, but one factor was constant: the children lacked some, if not all, of the readiness skills required to learn to read. Hence the initial learning was hard, and all the children felt easily frustrated. A parent cannot possibly have the detachment or patience to ride with the frustrations and set-backs that inevitably occur; nor does he have the specialized training required to teach a child with serious learning disabilities. In these cases it takes an objective outsider (preferably a professional) who has the detachment and trained skill to help these children over the initial hurdles. He can judge the proper balance between modifying the task so the child will finally meet success and encouraging him enough so that he will keep on trying. A child who is frustrated by his lack of aptitude in a given area may take it out on a parent by digging in his heels, whereas he would continue the game with a teacher with whom he has a different, less loaded relationship.

Most children with learning disabilities have developed some insecurity about themselves. Thus every parental suggestion is interpreted as meaning: "Mom has to help me so much, because I'm no good." The resultant feelings of anger and inadequacy interfere with *all* learning.

Getting Outside Help

If, for whatever reason, you have decided that you cannot teach your own preschool child, don't give up. If your child is a natural reader and wants to be taught (but not by you!), make the effort to find an outsider to teach him. If you have a child who finds the readiness skills hard to develop, find someone else who can work with him. The latter child is as important, even more important, than the former for a parent to understand and deal with. Like Bobby and Lisa he may have one or more learning disabilities which make learning sound-letter relationships and learning to read a difficult process. Such a child needs more time to learn than a natural reader; he should have that time when he is interested in letters, enjoys games, and has not yet developed the fear that he is not as good as his peers. Early intervention not only prevents his learning disabilities from escalating but increases his motivation to learn.

There are a number of alternatives if you decide that you cannot teach your own child, some of which we've touched on briefly in other chapters. Good preschools, if they include in their program a short but definite time for the development of structured readiness activities, are very helpful. Modified Montessori preschools are ideal provided they include in their program creative activities as well as individual instruction. Maria Montessori, an Italian educator, was one of the first to point out the tremendous satisfaction children gain from achievement in an intellectual area. Her conviction was that many children, free to choose, prefer work to play, because they enjoy the chal-

lenge of a purposeful, structured task. She believed that
the young child's sensitive periods for learning letters occur early, at four or five, that at that time his desire and
curiosity are at a peak and that he consequently thrives in
a learning environment structured for his needs. In a Montessori school many learning materials are displayed on
open shelves: a child can choose which games to play and
ask the teacher to help him with any new game that may
well involve learning letters or numbers.

Unfortunately, Montessori herself, as well as those followers who adhere very rigidly to her system, regards
block-building, painting, and free rhythms as unnecessary
frills. From my experience these experiences enhance a
child's reading readiness. He needs a chance to experiment in *all* areas. I would advise you to choose a modified
Montessori preschool which includes creative activities as
well as those that challenge a child's intellectual development.

Good kindergartens that have a readiness program
which includes teaching sound-letter knowledge are an excellent solution. If your child is a natural reader he will
thrive there.

If there is no suitable preschool or kindergarten available to you, your next decision depends on what kind of a
child you have. Perhaps he belongs in a class with the
natural reader and does not seem to have a serious learning problem. Suppose you are lucky enough to have an
extended family living close by: you might call on a grand-
parent, aunt, or uncle who would enjoy playing games
with your child and watching him learn.

Or you might consider hiring an interested high school
student. Most preschool children take to this particular
age group and enjoy attention from teenagers. Your local
high school principal (write for an appointment to see
him) is a good person to look to for help in choosing
someone for this job. Arrange a time with the student
when the two of you can go over the directions for playing
the games involved in reading readiness before he begins
teaching your child. He should know that each picture
must be identified correctly in all of the games and that
the child is to be taught a letter as recording the initial
sound of a meaningful, spoken word. Points to be empha-

sized are that the sound names of the letters, not the alphabet names, are to be used and that the games are self-corrective: if the child makes a mistake, the "teacher" does not have to say "wrong" but simply points to the correct letter picture.

If your child has learned all the letters and wants to learn to read, you need to take time out and explain the learning-to-read process to the young teacher. He must understand that he is not to teach your child to read by *telling* him what a word or sentence says in a book. Instead he should follow the method set forth in this book, confining himself to linguistically regular words only. By using the games, he will catch on to the essential principle: that the initial reading instruction is a learning process that a child can understand and use as a tool, and is not a series of words to be memorized.

Once teacher and pupil have experienced the excitement that comes from independent decoding, they won't need your guidance. Leave them alone and judge the success of the experiment by your child's reaction. As long as he continues to like having the student come, you are pretty safe. Don't ask him to evaluate his "teacher"; confine your supervision to direct discussion with the teacher later. Be willing to give this teenager time and understand that he, too, needs your approval and praise. The assumption is, of course, that you have picked a warm person who likes children and who has the necessary patience to teach them.

Schools for the Child with Learning Difficulties

Now let's consider how you would proceed with your child if he has learning difficulties. We will assume that you have recognized such difficulties after you and your child have worked through the initial material and he still has trouble remembering the name and shape of the first two letters. First of all, stop teaching him yourself and look for alternative solutions. There are several possibilities. If your child is about four years old, enriched Montessori preschools are ideal. If your child is five and goes to a public school kindergarten, find out if it offers a structured readiness program. Arrange for a conference with the kindergarten teacher early in the year to find out how

your child is getting along. If he is having learning difficulties, I would suggest one-to-one tutoring help, which
I'll outline below.

Should there neither be a good private preschool nor a
structured reading readiness program in a public school
kindergarten available for your child, you may want to
have his learning disabilities diagnosed by a psychologist,
a learning disabilities specialist, or a reading specialist.
You may want to know *before* the child experiences failure what kind of outside help is indicated. If only a slight
disability is found, look for the high school student discussed earlier. In one such instance I found a student willing to work during the summer with a child who was to
attend public school kindergarten in the fall. I had suggested half an hour every morning as a suitable beginning.
After two weeks the child insisted on playing games for
one hour.

If your child has learning disabilities in some areas and
you (and the expert) feel you need a trained person for the
job, look for a warm and accepting graduate student or a
teacher on leave of absence. Aside from liking children, he
or she must be convinced that teaching some of the sound-
letter correspondence before a child goes to school will
pay dividends in first grade. She must be willing to teach
him with games, as outlined in this book, and understand
the importance of allowing him to learn at his own pace.

Finally there is the possibility that the expert's evaluation will show that your child has specific learning disabilities. In this case I would recommend that your child be
tutored by a reading specialist to insure that he doesn't
experience failure when he goes to first grade. It makes
sense to tutor preschool children, for it takes *less* time and
less effort (and less money!) to prevent the damage this is
later so difficult to undo. In the next chapter I will present
reasons and evidence (excerpts from records of my own
pupils) how successful tutoring of preschool children
really is.

If your child is ready for first grade and has been receiv-
ing help from an outsider, I'd suggest a conference with
the tutor, the first grade teacher, and yourself to decide
whether the outside teaching can be discontinued. In my
own practice, I try to finish tutoring a preschool child by

the time he enters first grade. When this is not possible, I continue and cooperate closely with the first grade teacher.

If you should decide against teaching your child at any stage, you can be sure that you may still fill many other, perhaps more important needs. This point is nicely illustrated by a story told to me by a first grade teacher. It concerned a boy who had been taught to read at home while attending kindergarten. His teacher was happy that the boy could read and was glad when told that the teaching at home had terminated when he had entered first grade. One day the boy was asked to tell his mother to come to an important meeting that night. "Oh, but she can't come," he said. "Why not?" the teacher asked with a slight trace of suspicion. "Because we need her to cuddle us while we watch 'Disneyland,'" the boy explained.

11

A PLEA FOR EARLY INTERVENTION

It has been my experience that children with serious learning disabilities should be taught to read at four, so they can have two years to learn before they enter first grade. Thus they can at least partially overcome their difficulties *before* these difficulties are allowed to escalate in school. They need early private tutoring from a reading specialist who has the necessary training and experience to gauge how to adapt each learning task to the child without frustrating him, and yet still presenting him with a challenge.

Many parents and teachers at this point raise the question, "Why tutor a four-year-old? He is so young. He has plenty of time to learn . . ." The answer is that a number of these children can learn to read if they are given intensive tutoring by the middle or even the end of first grade. However, such a postponement of special help is risky. Since maturation in itself does not cure the disabilities, left alone the problems are compounded at the beginning of first grade. In a classroom situation a child who makes reversals such as writing a letter backward, or mirror writing, or reading words backward, cannot be corrected by the classroom teacher. Thus nine times out of ten he will carry out the error and reinforce tendencies which become ever more difficult to break.

Even under the most ideal first grade conditions, a warm, sympathetic, and accepting teacher, a nonthreatening classroom such as the open classroom, a totally relaxed and noncompetitive atmosphere emanating from both teacher and parent the child himself is the first to see that other children catch on more quickly and have progressed to readiness books or reading books while he is still struggling with the first letters. Feelings of inadequacy and failure damage his self-image and harm his natural motivation to learn. School becomes a place where "no matter how hard I try, I am not as good as the others." Willingness to try dwindles. Too often the learning pattern in first grade is set for the rest of his school years.

Having tutored preschool children as a preventive measure and also having done remedial work with school-age children, I vastly prefer the former. Even when a child has been referred to me as early as the middle of first grade, the job is more difficult since so many children already feel apprehensive and discouraged about their ability to learn. Moreover, parents, too, become apprehensive and communicate this uneasiness to the child, not necessarily through words. Thus a reading specialist is faced with the double job of remedying the lack of reading skills and also helping the child overcome his feelings of discouragement. In contrast, working with a very difficult preschool child who has not yet developed deep-seated negative feelings about his capacities is always easier. Hence my plea for early intervention.

Incidentally not only are children and parents spared frustration but so are first grade teachers. All of the classroom teachers I have worked with have been most appreciative that children with serious learning disabilities have come to first grade knowing how to read. Since these children feel successful in as crucial an area as reading, they are more patient and willing to try, e.g. learning math, where they will probably need more time and more effort than most of their classmates.

How will you know if your four-year-old child has serious learning disabilities and needs early tutoring? You won't really know without an outside evaluation. If your child shows some of the learning difficulties of my pupils discussed in the following case studies, then take your child to an expert for a professional diagnosis. Be sure to choose a learning disabilities specialist, a reading specialist, or a psychologist who knows that a child does not outgrow his learning difficulties naturally but needs systematic help to overcome them.

The following excerpts from my records present the strongest evidence for early intervention. Arlene, Bobby, and Lisa, who had serious learning disabilities, were tutored at four and, therefore, never experienced failure. Since they were able to learn to read through independent discovery, they enjoyed the learning process itself and developed confidence in their ability to learn and think. The children's comments will give you an understanding of how successful such children can feel.

Excerpt from Arlene's Record

Arlene came to me the summer before she entered public school kindergarten. She was not quite five. She was referred to me by a psychiatrist who was concerned that she had a very poor self-image and an extremely low frustration tolerance. In addition she had been diagnosed as having a serious perceptual problem. Because of these and other difficulties Arlene had had the unique misfortune of being "flunked out" of nursery school.

Arlene could not have been taught by her parents for many reasons. She had three older brothers and a younger one so close to her age that the rivalry between them was intense. No amount of parental attention seemed to have helped her feelings of jealousy and insecurity. Apart from the family structure, she was not an easy child to teach. At four-and-a-half she had developed such negative feelings about herself that she had a very low frustration tolerance. At the beginning of our sessions, she greeted every task with, "That's too hard. I can't do that." It took a lot of patience to teach Arlene, for I had to judge each time whether a task or a game was really too hard and should be simplified or whether with quiet but firm support Arlene could handle it. Yet Arlene not only learned to read before entering first grade, but when she realized that she could read new words on her own, she burst out, "Oh, I'm so clever!"

Excerpts from Bobby's Record

You will remember Bobby from chapter three as a child with tremendous learning problems. His parents, in particular, had noticed his poor motor coordination: he had difficulty catching a ball as well as holding a pencil. His mother realized early that she could not help her own child get ready for reading: "I wasn't able to teach him to hold a pencil . . . I had to back out. He was so resistant . . . He just won't listen to directions. He wears me down."

The father expressed his concern that Bobby would not try anything unless he could do it well.

Bobby and I started working together when he was four years and seven months. For two years we met once a week for an hour. Bobby's visual discrimination was slow in developing, slower than that of any other children whose records I use in this book. In the course of eight months Bobby really only *knew* eight letters, but he never felt discouraged about his learning. Because he was allowed to check each letter with its letter picture card rather than having to ask me for its name, he felt a sense of growing accomplishment which gave rise to a spurt in learning. He mastered the remaining sixteen letters in six months.

It has been my experience that this happens frequently with children with learning disabilities. It takes them a very long time to develop the visual discrimination necessary to identify letters. Once they have developed the skill and have understood the learning process, they get the hang of it. So they learn the remaining letters far more quickly.

Bobby, like most children with poor visual discrimination, felt most successful in writing. Because of all the tracing practice, he developed a kinesthetic feeling for a given letter: it was as if his muscle sense directed his hand in forming the letter, almost like learning Braille. Bobby's eagerness to practice writing and spelling helped him to finally master all the letters.

When Bobby came to reading words his poor visual discrimination again slowed up his initial progress. It took him three months to master (i.e. read fluently) the short-a words and two months to master the short-i words. No school could have afforded Bobby this much time to practice. Yet here, too, with concentrated practice, he learned to read these words fluently. Moreover, as he realized he was reading words without my help, he became increasingly confident. A year and a half after we started work every one of his comments show his feeling of competence. (I have put his age in parentheses before each comment so you can see the intervals at which his learning occurred.)

(6:0)

When Bobby completed a difficult page, he looked absolutely radiant: "I can say the words now. Boy, I am smart." (What he meant was: now I can read them in the same fast way as I am talking.)

Bobby refused help with a new word. "I want to be on my own. I don't like people helping me."

(6:2)

"These words are easy. You know, reading is so easy."

(6:3)

When he pressured me to start a new page, he said: "Let's go. You know I'm good at it. Here we go."

He worked steadily, again noting: "I figured it out all by myself."

Our final session ended with the following dialogue:
Bobby: "What do they do in first grade on the first day? Teach you how to read?"
Mrs. G.: "I don't think so."
Bobby: "It won't be hard for me when they do."

Excerpts from Lisa's Record

Lisa was brought to me at the age of four years and eleven months. Her parents reported that her early development had been slow. Lisa had been tested by a psychologist, and the IQ score on the performance test was markedly lower than the one obtained on the verbal test. Her combined score, from both verbal and motor tests, was average. I asked to see Lisa for two evaluating sessions.

I found that: 1) Lisa listened well; she was able to follow directions, and she obviously enjoyed the individual attention, encouragement, and praise. 2) Her attention and concentration span were excellent; she was not ready to go home after the full hour of either visit. 3) She moved quickly from not seeming able to hear initial sounds of words in the first session to being able to identify them in the second. 4) Lisa caught on well to new tasks, but she showed extremely poor eye-hand coordination, and her directional sense was weak; she traced every circle in the wrong direction, although I first demonstrated with my pencil which way to go.

It seemed to me that, like Bobby, Lisa could overcome a great many of her learning difficulties if someone worked carefully with her and allowed her to proceed at her own pace. In such a way she would not have any experiences of failure.

Not long after we had begun working together Lisa was tested in school and found to have a perceptual impairment. During her kindergarten year she was given special help in this area from an adjunct teacher two times a week.

Lisa was five years and two months when we began regular lessons. She appeared eager to work in the Readiness Book, which she remembered from our preliminary sessions. When Lisa spontaneously asked for a "new letter," I introduced the letter picture card for the [f]; remembering the learning process perfectly she said the word *fan* slowly to herself and then added, "So the letter says [f]."

For a long time Lisa had difficulty tracing a *m* in the correct direction. I gave her additional practice. She followed my finger tracing the *m*; then she traced it on her own with her finger several times; only then did she trace the dotted *m* with a crayon. Interestingly enough, she was about to start tracing the second *m* starting at the bottom and to the right when I stopped her and pointed with my

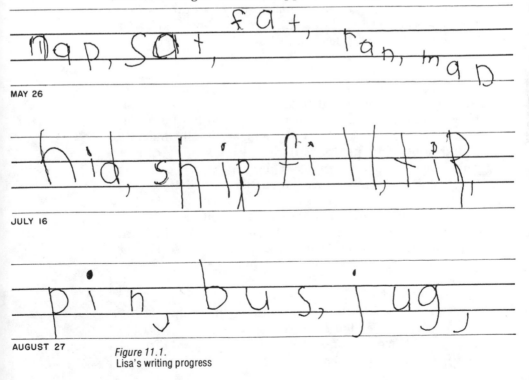

MAY 26

JULY 16

AUGUST 27

Figure 11.1.
Lisa's writing progress

finger to the beginning. For the next two months my finger would show Lisa where to start and thus prevent her, unobtrusively, from going in the wrong direction.

(5:5)

Lisa can identify ten letters and she is exuberant with her success. When I introduce the harder version of the Mailman Game to her, using plain letters instead of their letter picture cards, Lisa comments, "It's harder this way, but I can do anything I want to do."

Yet at this same time her tracing was still very poor. She enjoyed the Letter Writing Game, which was extremely difficult for her because it was embedded in a winning game. When I hesitate where to write my letter, Lisa teases: "I was faster. I'm pretty smart . . . smarter than you."

(5:6)

Lisa wants to try to write straight letters freehandedly without my dotting them for her first. "I can do it all by myself," she insisted. From this time on her motivation to learn increased by leaps and bounds.

(5:9)

Her motor coordination seems to have improved. Her lines are straighter and, therefore, I was able to show her how the letters are aligned with respect to the lines and spaces on the paper. Perceiving and accomplishing this is incredibly difficult for children like Lisa. She cannot remember which letter starts at the top, which occupies the middle, and which reaches to the bottom line. It is clear she will need many months to learn to align the letters properly. However, since there was no way for her to compare her performance with that of other children, she never felt defeated but was free to evaluate herself solely in relation to her own progress.

(5:10)

Lisa can read her first words without my help. During this memorable session Lisa would look at me from time to time with wonder and happiness: "I can read, Toni. I really can. Did you hear me?"

Her first writing of whole words shows that she had no difficulty in spelling them (see figure 11.1). Obviously, her only difficulty was in aligning the words properly in space. In fact, I dictated words which she had not yet been taught: *sat, fat, ran, mad*. By repeating the words to herself and slowly listening to each sound, she was able to write them by transfer, because she had thoroughly understood the encoding process. Lisa is very pleased at being able to write these words. "I can think it out," she comments.

(5:11)
There is a trend, from lesson to lesson, toward fuller and more significant definitions. Whereas in the beginning Lisa did not use full sentences, she now does. At one point when we played the Word Writing Game Lisa asked me: "Should I write a capital or a real one?" The implication that capitals are not real letters struck me as a delightful indication of her originality.

Her increased verbal facility was noticed at home. Her mother said, "Lisa talks about everything at home. She asks about everything. She just seems more intelligent."

(6:1)
Lisa's mother stopped in to report that Lisa is now trying to read everything in sight. Overnight she has begun asking her parents to tell her words which she cannot figure out by herself. A few days later Lisa spotted the date on my notes: "I can read it. It says August."

(6:2)
Lisa can write words without one spelling mistake and she can align the letters properly. Eleven months of constant writing practice was bearing fruit. Lisa's coordination had become stabilized, and her ability to align letters properly had become very much more reliable (see diagram 11.1 for her progress).

Lisa's improvement showed up in school, where a psychologist tested her again at the end of kindergarten. He no longer found a perceptual impairment and withdrew his original recommendation that Lisa be placed in a special first grade class for children with learning disabilities. Instead he recommended that Lisa be placed in a regular first grade.

What is as rewarding as Lisa's catching up and developing strength in her areas of weakness is her motivation to read. But because children like Lisa have lived with real success, they read constantly, as confirmed by the parents. The following dialogue proves this point:

Mrs. G.: "What do you like best in school?"
Lisa: "My teacher"
Mrs. G.: "And next best?"
Lisa: "The children."
Mrs. G.: "And next best?"
Lisa: "*Books.*"

CONCLUSION

To a healthy young child learning—including learning to read—is fun. If you teach a child to read so that he understands the learning process, his natural interest in reading is kindled. He enjoys learning because his mind is working, because he is active, not passive, in the learning process.

The decision of how to teach a child to read came from an examination of learning in general. Children learn most productively and economically through insight into structure: insight allows for transfer, for the excitement of being able to apply their learning to new tasks. Such learning is a challenge to the mind, not a burden to the memory.

In contrast, to learn by rote any subject that has a structure is unproductive. Memorization gives no opportunity for transfer; it simply means learning more facts in order to cover the material, rather than having a tool which would help in discovering new, related facts independently.

In reading a child can learn through understanding structure if the initial reading vocabulary is organized so that all of the initial words presented are linguistically regular. In the method outlined here, the initial instruction follows a highly structured sequence: from careful decoding, to fluent reading of single, linguistically regular words, to reading sentences. But within the structured sequence there is allowance for each child's active discovery and individual rate of learning.

Structural Reading can be adapted to suit the special needs of individual children. Children with poor auditory discrimination can have more time, more practice, and more enrichment activities in their area of weakness. Likewise children with poor visual discrimination are given all the time and practice and special activities they need in the initial phase of learning sound-letter correspondence to master the letters.

All children, bright as well as slow, do better in a learning system that is intellectually logical. The brighter the student, the more able he is to generalize and to transfer his reading skill to reading words he has not been taught before: i.e. the faster he will be able to read material of all kinds. Significantly, a less intelligent pupil also has done better with an approach that requires thinking rather than pure rote learning. By being able to reconstruct words on his own, which he may have forgotten, he achieves a feeling of confidence and security.

The bright child in our educational system is often neglected on the premise that "bright children will learn no matter what." True. Such a child may learn to read. But *how* he learns, in the very beginning of formal learning, will have as pronounced an effect on his subsequent intellectual development as it does on the slower child. If he learns to read in such a way that he can use his intellectual powers in the learning process itself, then he develops an increasing confidence that he is an able thinker, that he can apply his thinking to new tasks on his own, independent of the adult.

For many decades the word "method" has fallen into disrepute among many educators who have pointed out the priority of other factors in teaching and learning than the specific method used. This is, of course, absolutely valid for the teacher as well as for the parent. The personal qualities of the teacher and his intuitive handling of each individual child are far more important to the child's ultimate learning than any particular method. Similarly, the parent's attitude, his relationship with his child, is by far the single most significant underlying factor in the child's ability to learn. It takes a warm, sensitive parent to give his child challenge, not pressure, approval and support, not criticism. In an intellectual area, the young child must never be allowed to feel that he does not quite measure up to the parent's expectations.

Given these priorities method does assume its importance. A self-teaching approach to reading allows the child to venture forth on his own while the parent (or teacher) serves more in the capacity of a helping observer. If the child is taught with a method that lays visible the structure of the subject, he can learn through insight and thus develops, in the learning process itself, a steadily increasing confidence in his own ability to think.

As controversial as what method to use in teaching reading is the question of when to start. Youngsters benefit most from learning at that critical time when they are at a peak of readiness. The natural reader indicates in his curiosity about the printed language that he is ready to learn much sooner than our schools are prepared to teach him. He should not be kept waiting with the promise that "he will learn to read in first grade." If the critical period is missed, the child may lose some of his incentive to close the gap between his interest in the contents of books and his ability to read them himself. The bright youngster, at five, is simply interested in learning to read; at six he wants to read about rockets, the moon, or early pioneer days.

It is not safe to let a natural reader teach himself to read; on his own he may teach himself a reading skill that is imperfect. By nature children are impatient: it is quicker to guess at a word than to figure it out accurately. If you help your child discover reading, you can prevent the habit of guessing from developing. By giving your child the tools to unlock the meaning of a word accurately, you let him experience an excitement that far surpasses a hasty and haphazard stabbing at words.

The child who shows less interest in reading than the natural reader should also have an early start because he will require more preparation. By starting early you can take advantage of his pleasure in games and his need to have you spend time with him.

An early start in reading readiness is advisable for *all* children—not to satisfy a parent's ambitions but to gain time for your child to acquire some of the necessary readiness skills, including some sound-letter knowledge.

There are, at the other end of the continuum from the natural reader, children with such pronounced learning disabilities that only a professional can help them. Such early intervention is very successful. These children then are given the extra time and practice they need to learn to read: in this way they experience success rather than failure. Furthermore, the children's difficulties are corrected before they escalate in school.

Not only are children spared the ordeal of failing, but their parents are also spared the anguish of watching their child suffer when he is not able to learn in first grade. Moreover, first grade teachers are most appreciative when such a child comes to school knowing how to read.

I am not saying, of course that all reading problems would disappear if all children were taught early. There are children with such serious neurological or psychological impairments that they may not be able to learn to read.

Nor does my plea for an early start stem from a concern that four- and-five-year-olds do not accomplish enough. We can see from their comments how even children with learning problems, if started early enough, develop an increasing confidence not only in their reading skill but also in their thinking ability. They are aware that their intelligence is an important factor in learning to read.

A child should learn through thinking as early as possible, for it is the thinking, and not the amount learned, that will contribute to his intellectual growth. We should evaluate his knowledge by how well he can apply it in new situations or in tasks he has not been taught. Only in this way do we allow for creativity in the intellectual areas as we do naturally in the arts.

The child who is helped to figure out words on his own, to think out a sentence, practices thinking and will get better and better at it. And, in this process of learning to use his mind and discovering that he can depend on his ability to think, he develops an ever increasing motivation for learning more.

When five-year-old Lisa insisted that she no longer needed a certain teaching aid, she put it very succinctly: "I want the hard way. I like the thinking way . . . That's the way to learn."

Appendix I Learning Materials for Reading Readiness and Reading

Commercially available materials to help your child learn reading readiness and reading are contained in:

The Structural Reading Program
by Catherine Stern, Toni S. Gould, and Margaret B. Stern
published by Random House, Inc.
201 East 50th St.
New York, N.Y. 10022

The following components of this program can be ordered separately directly from the publisher:

We Discover Sounds and Letters (Book A-1)
One pupil's and one teacher's edition

More Sounds and Letters (Book A-2)
One pupil's and one teacher's edition

Key Picture Cards
One set

Sound-Picture Cards
One set. You must specify that this item is from the 1966 Structural Reading Series

We Discover Reading (Book B)
One pupil's and one teacher's edition

Dominoes for Book B
One set

Vocabulary Development Booklets for Book B
One set. Specify that this item is from the 1966 Structural Reading Series

We Read and Write (Book C)
One pupil's and one teacher's edition

Dominoes for Book C
One set

Vocabulary Development Booklets for Book C
One set. Specify that this item is from the 1966 Structural Reading Series

Is It So?
This is the first reader, which goes with Book C. Your child will enjoy reading it on his own.

Six and Six
This is the second reader, which goes with Book C. Your child will enjoy reading it by himself.

Appendix II Learning Materials for Number Readin

Materials to help your child learn number readiness and number concepts are contained in:

The Structural Arithmetic Program
by Catherine Stern, Margaret B. Stern, and Toni S. Gould
published by the Houghton Mifflin Co.
Pennington-Hopewell Road

Appendix III Bibliography for Parents

If you are interested in obtaining more information on how children learn, I recommend the following books:

Bruner, Jerome S. *The Process of Education.* Cambridge: Harvard University Press, 1962.

DeHirsch, Katrina; Jansky, Jeannette, J.; and Langford, William S. *Predicting Reading Failure.* New York: Harper & Row, 1966.

Durkin, Dolores. *Children Who Read Early. Two Longitudinal Studies.* New York: Teachers College Press, 1966.

Ginott, Haim G. *Between Parent and Child.* New York: Avon, 1969 (originally Macmillan, 1965).

Holt, John. *How Children Learn.* New York: Pitman Publishing Co., 1969.

Montessori, Maria. *The Discovery of the Child.* Translated by M. Joseph Castelloe. New York: Ballantine Books, 1972.

Parker, Ronald K. *The Pre-School in Action.* Boston: Allyn & Bacon, 1972.

Pines, Maya. *Revolution in Learning, the Years from Birth to Six.* New York: Harper & Row, 1966

Stone, L. Joseph, and Church, Joseph. *Childhood and Adolescence.* New York: Random House, 1973 (originally 1957).

Wadsworth, Barry J. *Piaget's Theory of Cognitive Development.* New York: David McKay Co., 1973.

White, Burton L. *The First Three Years of Life.* Englewood Cliffs, N.J.: Prentice Hall, 1975.

Winick, Mariann. *Before the 3 R's.* New York: David McKay Co., 1973.

Appendix IV A List of Picture Books
Without Texts for Young Children

Baran, Tancy. *Bees*. New York: Grosset & Dunlap Wonder Books, 1971.

Barner, Bob. *The Elephant's Visit*. Boston: Little, Brown & Co., (Atlantic Monthly Press), 1975.

Carroll, Ruth. *What Whiskers Did*. New York: Scholastic Book Services (StarLine Book), 1965.

Garth, Williams. *Baby Farm Animals*. Racine, Wisconsin: Western Publishing Co. (Golden Press), 1974, 18th printing.

————. *Baby's First Book*. Racine, Wisconsin: Western Publishing Co. (Golden Press), 1975, 7th printing.

Goddall, John S. *The Adventures of Paddy Pork*. New York: Harcourt, Brace Jovanovich, 1968.

————. *Shrewbellina's Birthday*. New York: Harcourt Brace Jovanovich, 1971.

Hamberger, John. *A Sleepless Day*. (paperback —StarLine) New York: Scholastic Book Services, 1975.

Hogrogian, Nonny. *Apples*. New York: Macmillan, 1972.

Hutchins, Pat. *Changes, Changes*. New York: Macmillan, 1971.

Mayer, Mercer. *Frog Goes to Dinner*. New York: The Dial Press, 1974.

Mayer, Mercer. *Bubble, Bubble*. New York: Parents Magazine Press, 1973.

————. *A Boy, A Dog, A Frog And A Friend*. Eau Claire, Wisconsin: E.M. Hale, 1972.

Richetts, Michael. *Rain*. New York: Grosset & Dunlap (Wonder Books), 1974.

Starr, Christine. *Clothes*. New York: Grosset & Dunlap (Wonder Books), 1971.

————. *Homes*. Wonder Books. New York: Grosset & Dunlap (Wonder Books), 1971.

————. *Milk*. New York: Grosset & Dunlap (Wonder Books), 1971.

Wegel, Peter. *The Naughty Bird*. Chicago: The Follett Publishing Co., 1967.

Appendix V A List of Books to Read Aloud to Childr from Two to Five Years of Age

Adkins, Jan. *Inside: Seeing Beneath the Surface.* New York: Walker & Co., 1975.

Adorjan, Aarol Madden. *Someone I Know.* New York: Random House (Early Bird), 1968.

Alexander, Martha. *I'll Be the Horse If You'll Play with Me.* New York: The Dial Press, 1975.

Andry, Andrew C., and Kratka, Suzanne. *Hi, New Baby.* New York: Simon & Schuster, 1970.

Ardizzone, Aingelda. *The Night Ride.* New York: E. P. Dutton (Windmill Books), 1975.

d'Aulaire, Ingri, and Edgar. *Abraham Lincoln.* New York: Doubleday, 1939.

Barrett, Judi. *I Hate To Take a Bath.* New York: Scholastic Book Services (Four Winds Press), 1975.

Baylor, Byrd. *Before You Came This Way.* New York: E. P. Dutton, 1969.

Becker, John. *Seven Little Rabbits.* New York: Walker & Co., 1975.

Belting, Natalia. *Winter's Eve.* New York: Holt, Rinehart & Winston, 1969.

Bemelmans, Ludwig. *Madeline in London* (and other Madeline books) New York: Viking Press, 1972 (orig. 1939).

Bennett, Vivian. *My Tell Time Book* (and others) New York: Grosset & Dunlap, 1975.

Berends, Polly Berrien. *Who's That In The Mirror, Polly?* New York: Random House (Early Bird), 1968.

Boegehold, Betty. *What The Wind Told.* New York: Parents Magazine Press, 1974.

Bond, Jean Carey. *Brown Is a Beautiful Color.* New York: Franklin Watts, 1969.

Borea, Phyllis. (photography by Raimondo Borea) *First Thing in the Morning.* New York: Cowles Book Co., 1970.

Bremburg, Petronella. *Shawn Goes to School.* New York: Thomas Y. Crowell Co., 1973.

Brenner, Barbara. *Cunningham's Rooster.* New York: Parents Magazine Press, 1975.

Bright, Robert. *Me and the Bears.* Garden City, N.Y.: Doubleday, 1951.

Brown, Marcia. *How Hippo.* New York: Charles Scribner's Sons, 1969.

Brown, Margaret Wise. *Winter Noisy Book* (and all the other Noisy Books) New York: Harper & Row, 1947.

————. *Wonderful Story Book.* Racine: Wisconsin, Western Publishing Co. (Golden Press), 1974.

————. *Goodnight Moon.* New York: Harper & Row, 1947.

————. *Wait Till The Moon Is Full.* New York; Harper & Row, 1948.

————. *The Runaway Bunny.* New York: Franklin Watts, 1963.

————. *Steamroller.* New York: Walker & Co., 1974.

Budney, Blossom. *After Dark.* New York: Lothrop, Lee and Shepard Co., 1975.

Burningham, John. *The Gumpy's Outing.* New York: Holt, Rinehart & Winston, 1970.

Burton, Virginia Lee. *The Little House.* Boston: Houghton Mifflin Co., 1969 (orig. 1943).

Caldecott, Randolph. *Hey Diddle Diddle.* New York: Frederick Warne & Co., reprint of 1882 ed.

Chaffin, Lillie D. *Bear Weather.* New York: Macmillan, 1969.

Charlip, Remy. *Arm in Arm.* New York: Parents Magazine Press, 1969.

Clark, Bettina, with Dr. Lester L. Coleman. *Going To The Hospital.* New York: Random House (Pop-Up), 1971.

Clifton, Lucille. *Good, Says Jerome.* New York: E. P. Dutton, 1973.

Coatsworth, Elizabeth. *Mouse Chorus.* New York: Pantheon, 1955.

Cohen, Carol. *Wake Up, Groundhog!* New York: Crown Publishers, 1975.

Collodi, Carlo. *Adventures of Pinocchio.* New York: Macmillan, 1963.

Conford, Ellen. *Just the Thing for Geraldine.* Boston: Little, Brown and Co., 1974.

Daly, Kathleen N., *Four Little Kittens.* Racine, Wisconsin: Western Publishing Co. (Golden Press), 1974.

De Angeli, Marguerite. *Book of Nursery and Mother Goose Rhymes.* Garden City, N. Y.: Doubleday, 1954.

De Ball Kwitz, Mary. *When It Rains.* Chicago: The Follett Publishing Co., 1974.

DeBrunhoff, Jean. *The Story of Barbar* (and other Barbar Books) New York: Random House, 1933.

de Regniers, Beatrice Schenk. *The Giant Story.* New York: Harper & Row, 1953.

de Regniers, Beatrice ————. *What Can You Do With a Shoe?* New York: Harper & Row, 1955.

————. *May I Bring A Friend?* New York: Atheneum, 1964.

Dr. Seuss. *The Shape of Me and Other Stuff.* New York: Random House, 1973.

Duvoisin, Roger. *See What I Am.* New York: Lothrop, Lee and Shepard Co., 1974.

Eastman, P. D. *Everything Happens to Aaron.* New York: Random House, 1967.

————. *Big Dog, Little Dog.* New York: Random House, 1973.

Elmer, Irene. *A Lodestone and a Toadstone.* New York: Alfred A. Knopf, 1969.

Evers, Alf. *The Brave Little Steam Shovel.* New York: Wonder Books, 1974.

Fatio, Louise, and Duvoisin, Roger. *Marc and Pixie.* New York: McGraw-Hill Book Co., 1975.

Fisher, Aileen. *Listen, Rabbit.* New York: Thomas Y. Crowell Co., 1964.

Fisher, Aileen. *Once We Went On a Picnic.* New York: Thomas Y. Crowell Co., 1975.

Flack, Marjorie. *Angus and the Ducks.* Garden City, N. Y.: Doubleday, 1930.

Flack, Marjorie, and Wiese, Kurt. *The Story of Ping.* New York: The Viking Press, 1933.

Frank, Josette, ed. *Poems to Read to the Very Young.* New York: Random House, 1961.

Fraydas, Stan. *Hoppy, the Curious Kangaroo.* New York: Grosset & Dunlap (Wonder Books), 1974.

Friedman, Joy. T. *Look Around and Listen.* New York: Grosset & Dunlap, 1974.

Garelick, May. *What's Inside? The Story of an Egg That Hatched.* New York: Scholastic Book Services (StarLine), 1970.

————. *Where Does the Butterfly Go When It Rains?* New York: Scholastic Book Services (StarLine), 1961.

Gergely, Tibor. *Busy Day, Busy People.* New York: Random House, 1972.

Goff, Beth. *Where Is Daddy?: The Story of a Divorce.* Boston: Beacon Press, 1969.

Goodall, John S. *The Adventures of Paddy Pork.* New York: Harcourt Brace Jovanovich, 1968.

Graham, Margaret Bloy. *Be Nice to Spiders.* New York: Harper & Row, 1967.

Grimm, Jacob and Wilhelm. *The Shoemaker and the Elves.* New York: Charles Scribner's Sons, 1960.

Hartelius, Margaret E. *The Chicken's Child.* Garden City, N. Y.: Doubleday, 1975.

Hazen, Barbara. *The Tiny Tawny Kitten.* Racine, Wisconsin: Western Publishing Co. (Golden Press), 1975.

Hefter, Richard. *A noise in the closet.* (strawberry book and other books in this series) New York: Larousse & Co., 1974.

Hoban, Russell. *A Baby Sister for Frances.* New York: Harper & Row, 1964.

Hoban, Russell, and Hoban, Lillian. *Best Friends for Frances.* New York: Harper & Row, 1969.

————. *Bedtime For Frances.* New York: Harper & Row, 1960.

————. *Bread and Jam for Frances.* New York: Harper & Row, 1964.

Hoban, Russell, *Dinner at Alberto's.* New York: Thomas Y. Crowell Co., 1975.

Hoban, Tana. *Where Is It?* New York: Macmillan, 1974.

————. *over, under and through.* New York: Macmillan, 1973.

————. *Push Pull, Empty Full.* New York: Macmillan, 1972.

Hoffmann, Hilde. *The City and Country Mother Goose.* New York: McGraw-Hill, 1969.

Hoffman, Phyllis. *Steffee and Me.* New York: Harper & Row, 1970.

Holl, Addelaide. *Have You Seen My Puppy?* New York: Random House (Early Bird), 1968.

Hornblow, Leonora and Arthur. *Reptiles Do the Strangest Things.* New York: Random House, 1970.

Hughes, Langston. *The Dream Keeper and Other Poems.* New York: Alfred A. Knopf, 1932.

Hurd, Edith Thacher. *Catfish and the Kidnapped Cat.* New York: Harper & Row, 1974.

Hutchins, Pat. *The Surprise Party.* New York: Macmillan, 1969.

———. *Rosie's Walk.* New York: Macmillan, 1968.

———. *Changes. Changes.* New York: Macmillan, 1971.

———. *The Wind Blew.* New York: Macmillan, 1974.

Jewell, Nancy. *Calf, Goodnight.* New York: Harper & Row, 1973.

Joslin, Sesyle. *What Do You Say, Dear?* New York: William R. Scott, 1958.

Keats, Ezra Jack. *My Dog Is Lost.* New York: Thomas Y. Crowell Co., 1960.

———. *The Snowy Day.* New York: Viking Press, 1960.

———. *Whistle for Willie.* New York: Viking Press, 1964.

———. *Jennie's Hat.* New York: Harper & Row, 1966.

———. *Peter's Chair.* New York: Harper & Row, 1967.

———. *Goggles.* New York: Collier Books, 1969.

———. *Hi Cat!* (paperback) New York: Collier Books, 1970.

———. *Pet Show.* (paperback) New York: Collier Books, 1972.

———. *Pssst! Doggie.* New York: Franklin Watts, 1973.

———. *Dreams.* New York: Macmillan, 1974.

———. *Louie.* New York: William and Morrow Co. (Greenwillow), 1975.

Kesselman, Wendy. *Time for Jody.* New York: Harper & Row, 1975.

Krasilowsky, Phyllis. *The Very Little Girl.* New York: Doubleday, 1962.

————. *The Very Little Boy*. New York: Doubleday, 1962.

Kraus, Robert. *Leo the Late Bloomer*. New York: Windmill Books, 1971.

Krauss, Ruth. *The Happy Day*. New York: Harper & Row, 1949.

————. *A Very Special House*. New York: Harper & Row, 1953.

————. *A Hole Is to Dig: A First Book of First Definitions*. New York: Harper & Row, 1952.

————. *The Birthday Party*. New York: Harper & Row, 1957.

La Fontaine. *The Hare and the Tortoise*. New York: Franklin Watts, 1966.

Levine, Joan G. *A Bedtime Story*. New York: E. P. Dutton, 1975.

Libbey, Ruth E. *The Picnic at the Zoo*. New York: Grosset & Dunlap (Wonder Books), 1974.

Lionni, Leo. *Alexander and the Wind-Up Mouse*. New York: Pantheon, 1969.

————. *Fish is Fish*. New York: Pantheon, 1970.

Livingston, Myra Cohn. *I'm Hiding*. New York: Harcourt Brace Jovanovich, 1961.

Low, Joseph. *There Was a Wise Crow*. New York: Scholastic Book Services (StarLine), 1972.

MacDonald, George. *The Light Princess*. New York: Farrar, Strauss, and Giroux, 1969.

————. *The Golden Key*. New York: Farrar, Strauss, and Giroux, 1967.

Martin, Janet. *Round and Square*. New York: Platt and Munk Publ. Co., 1965.

Mayer, Mercer. *There's a Nightmare in My Closet*. New York: The Dial Press, 1968.

————. *What Do You Do With a Kangaroo?* New York: Scholastic Book Services (StarLine), 1975.

Max, Peter. *Peter Max Land of Yellow*. New York: Franklin Watts, 1970.

McCloskey, Robert. *Make Way for Ducklings*. New York: Viking Press, 1969 (orig. 1941).

———. *Blueberries for Sal.* New York: Viking Press, 1948.

Merriam, Eve. *Mommies At Work.* New York: Scholastic Book Services, 1955.

Miller, A. G. *POP-UP Sound-Alikes.* (Pop-Up Books and other books in this series) New York: Random House, 1967.

Milne, A. A. *Winnie-The-Pooh* (and others) New York: E. P. Dutton, 1926.

———. *When We Were Very Young.* New York: E. P. Dutton, 1924.

———. *Now We Are Six.* New York: E. P. Dutton, 1927.

Minarik, Else Holmelund. *No Fighting. No Biting.* New York: Harper & Row, 1958.

Mitchell, Donald., compiled and arranged by Carey Blyton. *Every Child's Book of Nursery Songs.* New York: Crown Publishers, 1968.

Mizumura, Kazue. *If I Were a Cricket.* New York: Thomas Y. Crowell Co., 1973.

Morton, Lois. *Let's Find Charlie.* New York: Random House, 1969.

Munari, Bruno. *Circus in the Mist.* New York: Collins-World, 1969.

Ness, Evaline. *Sam, Bangs and Moonshine.* New York Holt, Rinehart, & Winston, 1966.

Newberry, Clare Turlay. *April's Kittens.* New York: Harper & Row, 1940.

———. *Marshmallow.* New York: Harper & Row, 1942

Nicklaus, Carol, illus. *Can You Find What's Missing?* (Sesame Street Pop-Up Book Set and other books in this series) New York: Random House, 1974.

Nodset, Joan L. *Who Took the Farmer's Hat?* New York: Scholastic Book Services (StarLine), 1963.

Ormondroyd, Edward. *Theodore.* Berkeley, California: Parnassus Press, 1966.

Perkins, Al. *The Ear Book.* (Bright and Early Books and other books in this series) New York: Random House, 1968.

Potter, Beatrix. *The Tale of Peter Rabbit* (and other books by her). New York: Frederick Warne & Co., 1902.

Preston, Edna Mitchell. *The Temper Tantrum Book.* New York: Viking Press, 1969.

Reed, Zwendalyn ed. *Songs A Sandman Sings.* New York: Atheneum, 1969.

Reiss, John J. *Colors.* New York: Bradbury Press, 1969.

Rockwell, Anne. *Gift for a Gift.* New York: Parents Magazine Press, 1974.

————. *The Three Bears and Fifteen Other Stories.* New York: Thomas Y. Crowell Co., 1975.

Scarry, Patricia. *The Sweet Smell of Christmas.* New York: Golden Press, 1970.

Scarry, Richard. *What Do People Do All Day?* New York: Random House, 1968.

————. *Great Big Schoolhouse.* New York: Random House, 1969.

Sendak, Maurice. *Where the Wild Things Are.* New York: Harper & Row, 1963.

————. *In the Night Kitchen.* New York: Harper & Row, 1970.

Sesame Street. *What Happens Next?* (Sesame Street Pop-Up) New York: Random House, 1971.

————. *IN and OUT.* (A Book of Pop-Up Opposites) New York: Random House, 1971.

————. *The Ring on a Swing.* (Sesame Street Pop-Up) New York: Random House, 1972.

————. *Who Are the People in Your Neighborhood?* (Sesame Street Pop-Up) New York: Random House, 1974.

————. *Can You Find What's Missing?* (Sesame Street Pop-Up) New York: Random House, 1974.

Shapur, Fredun. *Round and Round and Square.* New York: Abelard Schuman, 1965.

Silverstein, Shel. *The Giving Tree.* New York: Harper & Row, 1964.

Skorpen, Liesel Moak. *Michael.* New York: Harper & Row, 1975.

Spier, Peter. *And So My Garden Grows.* Garden City, N. Y.: Doubleday, 1969.

Steig, William. *Sylvester and the Magic Pebble.* New York: Simon & Schuster, 1969.

Stein, Sara Bonnett. *That New Baby.* New York: Walker & Co., 1974.

Steptoe, John. *Stevie.* New York: Harper & Row, 1969.

Swift, Hildegarde H., and Ward, Lynd. *The Little Red Lighthouse and the Great Gray Bridge.* New York: Harcourt Brace Jovanovich, 1942.

Tarcov, Edith H. (retold from Grimm) *The Frog Prince.* New York: The Four Winds Press, 1974.

Turkle, Brinton. *Thy Friend, Obadiah.* New York: Viking Press, 1972.

Udry, Janice May. *A Tree Is Nice.* New York: Harper & Row, 1956.

————. *Let's Be Enemies.* New York: Harper & Row, 1961.

————. *The Mean Mouse and Other Mean Stories.* New York: Harper & Row, 1962.

————. *What Mary Jo Wanted.* Chicago: Albert Whitman Co., 1968.

Van Leeuwen, Jean. *Timothy's Flower.* New York: Random House, 1967.

Ving, Henry Ritchel. *What is big?* New York: Holt, Rinehart & Winston (Little Owl), 1963.

Viorst, Judith and Chrao, Kay. *My Mamma says.* New York: Atheneum, 1974.

Ward, Lynd. *The Biggest Bear.* Boston: Houghton Mifflin Co., 1952.

Warburg, Sandol Stoddard *Growing Time.* Boston: Houghton Mifflin Co., 1969.

Weigle, Oscar. *The Ugly Duckling.* (A Puppet *Storybook* and other books in this series) New York: Grosset & Dunlap, 1971.

————. *My Best Friends.* (. Preschool Puppet Book and other books in this series) New York: Grosset Dunlap, 1972.

Weil, Lisl. *Ralphi Rhino.* New York: Walker & Co., 1975.

Wells, Rosemary. *Morris's Disappearing Bag.* New York: The Dial Press, 1975

Werner, Jane (ed.) *The Golden Book of Poetry.* New York: Golden Press, 1969.

Wilde, George and Irma. *The Puppy Who Found a Boy.* Grosset & Dunlap, Inc. (Wonder Books), 1974.

Wilder, Laura Ingalls. *The Little House in the Big Woods* (and the sequels to this volume). New York: Harper & Row, 1932.

Zemach, Harve and Margot. *The Judge: An Untrue Tale.* New York: Farrar, Strauss, and Giroux, 1969.

Zindel, Paul. *I Love My Mother.* New York: Harper & Row, 1975.

Zolotow, Charlotte. *Mr.*

Rabbit and the Lovely Present. New York: Harper & Row, 1962.

––––––. *My Friend John.* New York: Harper & Row, 1968.

––––––. *The Summer Night.* New York: Harper & Row, 1974.

––––––. *When the Wind Stops.* New York: Harper & Row, 1975.

Appendix VI A list of Books for Beginning Readers

In general, I would recommend the Harper & Row *I CAN READ* Series, the Random House *Beginner Books,* the Thomas Y. Crowell *Let's-Read-and-Find-Out Science Books,* the Lippincott *Super Books,* the Western Publishing Company *Electric Co. Easy Easy Reader Golden Books.*

For easy-to-read, high quality paperbacks, I would recommend you get catalogs from the following publishers:

StarLine Books
Scholastic Book Services
Englewood Cliffs, N.J. 07632

Reader's Digest Service
Education Division
Pleasantville, N.Y. 10570

Dell Publishing Co.
1 Dag Hammerskjold Plaza
245 East 47th St.
New York, N.Y. 11017

Viking Paperbound Books
625 Madison Avenue
New York, N.Y. 10022

The following list of easy-to-read books is compiled from children's choices. Naturally not all of these books can be read by every beginning reader. If your child likes a specific book too difficult for him to read by himself, then read it to him. Some time later he will read it on his own.

Anglund, Joan Walsh. *What Color Is Love?* (and others). New York: Harcourt Brace Jovanovich, 1966.

Austin, Margot. *Barney's Adventure.* New York: Scholastic Book Services (StarLine), 1975.

Banner, Angela. *Ant and Bee Time* (and others). New York: Franklin Watts, 1969.

Batherman, Muriel. *Big and Small, Short and Tall.* New York: Scholastic Book Services (StarLine), 1975.

Benchley, Nathaniel. *Oscar Otter.* New York: Harper & Row (I Can Read Book), 1966.

Berenstain, Stanley and Janice. *The Bear Scouts.* New York: Random House (Beginner Book), 1967.

———. *The Bear Scouts.* New York: Random House (Beginner Book), 1970.

———. *The Bears' Picnic.* New York: Random House (Beginner Book), 1966.

———. *The Big Honey Hunt.* New York: Random House (Beginner Book), 1962.

———. *The Bike Lesson* New York: Random House (Beginner Book), 1964.

Boegehold, Betty. *Three to Get Ready.* New York: Harper & Row (I Can Read Book), 1965.

Bonsall, Crosby. *Who's a Pest?* New York: Harper & Row (I Can Read Book), 1962.

Branley, Franklin M. *Roots are Food Finders.* New York: Thomas Y. Crowell Co. (A Let's-Read-and-Find-Out Science Book), 1975.

———. *Light and Darkness.* New York: Thomas Y. Crowell Co. (A Let's-Read-and-Find-Out Science Book), 1975.

Brenner, Barbara. *Baltimore Orioles*. New York: Harper & Row (Science I CAN READ Book), 1974.

Bridwell, Norman. *The Witch Next Door*. New York: The Four Winds Press, 1966.

———. *A Tiny Family*. New York: Scholastic Book Services (StarLine), 1972.

———. *Bird in the Hat*. New York: Scholastic Book Services (StarLine), 1964.

———. *Clifford The Big Red Dog*. New York: Scholastic Book Services (StarLine), 1966.

———. *Clifford Gets a Job*. New York: Scholastic Book Services, (StarLine), 1972.

———. *The Country Cat*. New York: Scholastic Book Services (StarLine), 1971.

Brown, Margaret Wise. *The Little Fireman*. New York: Scholastic Book Services (StarLine), 1973.

Burningham, John. *The Baby*. New York: Thomas Y. Crowell Co. (John Burningham's Little Books), 1975.

———. *The Snow*. New York: Thomas Y. Crowell Co. (John Burningham's Little Books), 1975.

———. *The Rabbit*. New York: Thomas Y. Crowell Co. (John Burningham's Little Books), 1975.

———. *The School*. New York: Thomas Y. Crowell Co. (John Burningham's Little Books), 1975.

Carle, Eric. *The Mixed-Up Chameleon*. New York: Thomas Y. Crowell Co., 1975.

Cerf, Bennett. *Bennett Cerf's Book of Laughs*. New York: Random House (Beginner Book), 1959.

———. *Bennett Cerf's Book of Riddles*. New York: Random House (Beginner Book), 1960.

———. *More Riddles*. New York: Random House (Beginner Book), 1961.

———. *Bennett Cerf's Book of Animal Riddles*. New York: Random House (Beginner Book), 1964.

Chalmers, Audrey. *Hundreds and Hundreds of Pancakes*. New York: Viking Press, 1942.

Dr. Seuss. *The Cat in the Hat.* New York: Random House (Beginner Book), 1957.

———. *The Cat in the Hat Comes Back.* New York: Random House (Beginner Book), 1958.

———. *Green Eggs and Ham.* New York: Random House (Beginner Book), 1960.

———. *One Fish Two Fish Red Fish Blue Fish.* New York: Random House (Beginner Book), 1960.

———. *Hop on Pop.* New York: Random House (Beginner Book), 1963.

———. *Fox in Socks.* New York: Random House (Beginner Book), 1965.

De Witt, Johanna. *The Littlest Reindeer.* New York: The Children's Press, 1961.

Eastman, P. D. *Sam and the Firefly.* New York: Random House (Beginner Book), 1958.

———. *Are You My Mother?* New York: Random House (Beginner Book), 1960.

———. *Go, Dog, Go!* New York: Random House (Beginner Book), 1961.

———. *The Best Nest.* New York: Random House (Beginner Book), 1968.

———, and McKie, Roy. *Snow.* New York: Random House (Beginner Book), 1962.

Elkin, Benjamin. *The King's Wish and Other Stories.* New York: Random House, (Beginner Book), 1968.

———. *The Big Jump and Other Stories.* (Random House Beginner Book) New York: Random House (Beginner Book), 1968.

———. *Six Foolish Fishermen* New York: Scholastic Book Services (StarLine), 1968.

Farley, Walter. *Little Black, a Pony.* New York: Random House (Beginner Book), 1961.

———. *Little Black Goes to the Circus.* New York: Random House (Beginner Book), 1963.

Finfer, Celenthe; Wasserburg, Esther; and Winberg, Florence. *Grandmother Dear.* Chicago: Follett Publishing Co., 1957.

Flack, Marjorie. *Wait For William.* Boston: Houghton Mifflin Co., 1935.

———. *The Story About Ping.* New York: Viking Press, 1970.

Freeman, Don. *Mop Top.* New York: Viking Press, 1955.

Friskey, Margaret. *Indian Two Feet and His Horse.* New York: Children's Press, 1959.

Getz, Arthur. *Hamilton's Duck Springtime Story.* New York: Golden Press, 1974.

Gould, Toni S., and Teague, Kathleen. *Is It So?* (Reader of Structural Reading Program) New York: Random House, 1972.

———. *Six and Six.* (Reader of Structural Reading Program) New York: Random House, 1972.

———. *Hide and Seek.* (Reader of Structural Reading Program) New York: Random House, 1972.

———. *Just Think How Much.* (Reader of Structural Reading Program) New York: Random House, 1972.

Guilfoile, Elizabeth. *Nobody Listens to Andrew.* New York: Scholastic Book Services (StarLine), 1973.

Hawes, Judy. *Spring Peepers.* New York: Thomas Y. Crowell Co. (Let's-Read-and-Find-Out Science Book), 1975.

Heide, Florence, and Van Clief, Sylvia. *That's What Friends Are For.* New York: Scholastic Book Services (StarLine), 1968.

Heilbroner, Joan. *The Happy Birthday Present.* New York: Harper & Row (I Can Read Book), 1961.

Hoban, Lillian. *Arthur's Honey Bear.* New York: Harper & Row (I Can Read Book), 1974.

Hoban, Russell. *A Bargain for Frances.* New York: Harper & Row (I Can Read Book), 1970.

———. *Harvey's Hideout.* New York: Scholastic Book Services (StarLine), 1972.

———. *Tom and the Two Handles.* New York: Harper & Row (I Can Read Book), 1965.

Hoff, Syd. *Berkeley.* New York: Harper & Row (I Can Read Book), 1975.

Hurd, Edith Thatcher. *Hurry Hurry.* New York: Harper & Row (I Can Read Book), 1960.

Johnson, Crockett. *Harold and the Purple Crayon.* New York: Harper & Row, 1955.

Lobel, Arnold, *Frog and Toad Are Friends.* New York: Harper & Row (I Can Read Book), 1970.

———. *Frog and Toad Together.* New York: Harper & Row (I Can Read Book), 1972.

———. *Owl at Home.* New York: Harper & Row (I Can Read Book), 1975.

Low, Alice. *Summer.* New York: Random House (Beginner Book), 1963

Lustig, Loretta. *Where Does the Garbage Go?* New York: Thomas Y. Crowell Co. (A Let's-Read-and-Find-Out Book), 1974.

Mallett, Anne. *The Secret Kitten.* (paperback-StarLine) New York: Scholastic Book Services (StarLine), 1974.

Merriam, Eve. *Do You Want to See Something?* New York: Scholastic Book Services (StarLine), 1969.

Meyers, Bernice. *Not This Bear.* New York: Scholastic Book Services (StarLine), 1971.

Minarik, Else Holmelund. *No Fighting, No Biting!* New York: Harper & Row (I Can Read Book), 1958.

———. *Father Bear Comes Home.* New York: Harper & Row (I Can Read Book), 1959.

———. *Little Bear's Friends.* New York: Harper & Row (I Can Read Book), 1960.

———. *A Kiss for Little Bear.* New York: Harper & Row (I Can Read Book), 1968.

Mizumura, Kazue. *The Blue Whale.* New York: Thomas Y. Crowell Co. (A Let's-Read-and-Find-Out Science Book), 1971.

———. *Opossum.* New York: Thomas Y. Crowell Co. (A Let's-Read-and-Find-Out Science Book), 1974.

Moore, Lillian. *Junk Day* York: Parents Magazine Press, 1968.

Morris, Robert A. *Seahorse* New York: Harper & Row (Science I Can Read Book) 1972.

———. *Dolphin.* New York Harper & Row (Science I Can Read Book), 1975.

Obilgado, Lillian. *Sad Day Glad Day.* New York: Scholastic Book Services (StarLine), 1970.

Parish, Peggy. *Play Ball, Amelia Bedelia.* New York: Harper & Row (I Can Read Book), 1972.

Parnall, Peter. *Twist, Wiggle, and Squirm.* New York: Thomas Y. Crowell Co. (A Let's-Read-and-Find-Out Book), 1973.

Patrick, Gloria. *A Bug in a Jug and Other Funny Poems.* New York: Scholastic Book Services (StarLine), 1972.

Pringle, Laurence. *Water Plants.* New York: Thomas Y. Crowell Co. (A Let's-Read-and-Find-Out-Book), 1975.

Rand, Ann and Paul. *Sparkle and Spin.* New York: Harcourt Brace Jovanovich, 1957.

Riccuiti, Edward R. *An Animal for Alan.* New York: Harper & Row (I Can Read Book), 1970.

Scherer, Julian. *Upside Down Day.* Holiday House.

Selsam, Millicent E. *Hidden Animals.* New York: Harper & Row (Science I Can Read Book), 1969.

————. *Seeds and More Seeds.* New York: Harper & Row (Science I Can Read Book), 1959.

Sendak, Maurice. *Chicken Soup with Rice.* New York: Harper & Row, 1962.

Shapp, Martha and Charles. *Let's Find Out What the Signs Say* (and other books by these authors). New York: Franklin Watts, 1959.

Singer, Susan. *Kenny's Monkey.* New York: Scholastic Book Services (StarLine), 1969.

Skorpen, Liesel Moak. *Outside My Window.* New York: Harper & Row, 1968.

Smith, Mary and R. A. *Crocodiles Have Big Teeth All Day.* Chicago: Follett Publishing Co., 1970.

Sonneborn, Ruth A. *Seven in a Bed.* New York: Viking Press, 1968.

Vinton, Iris. *Look Out for Pirates.* New York: Random House (Beginner Book), 1961.

Weatherbee, Robert Francis. *The Boy Who Would Not Go to School.* New York: Scholastic Book Services (StarLine), 1975.

Wiseman, B. *Morris the Moose Goes to School.* New York: Scholastic Book Services, (StarLine) 1970.

Woods, Betty. *My Box and String.* New York: Scholastic Book Services (StarLine), 1970.

Zion, Gene. *Harry and the Lady Next Door.* New York: Harper & Row (I Can Read Book), 1960.

Appendix VII Children's Magazines

Some magazines have alphabet games which I do not recommend.

Child Life (Preschool–grade 6)
> 1110 Waterway Blvd.
> Indianapolis,
> Indiana 46206

Cricket
> Open Court Publ. Co.
> 1058 Eighth St.
> La Salle,
> Illinois 61301

Ebony, Jr. (A magazine written for black children)
> 1320 South Michigan Avenue
> Chicago,
> Illinois 60616

Electric Company Magazine
> Dept. S.O.–9
> North Road
> Poughkeepsie,
> New York 12601

Highlights for Children (ages two to twelve)
> 2300 West Fifth Avenue
> Columbus,
> Ohio 43216

Humpty Dumpty's Magazine for Little Children (excellent for beginning readers)
> Bergenfield,
> New Jersey 07621

Jack and Jill (ages 5–12)
> 1110 Waterway Blvd
> Indianapolis,
> Indiana 46206

Kids by Kids for Kids (ages 5 to fifteen; written by children)
> Kids' Publishers Inc.
> 777 Third Avenue
> New York,
> New York 10017

Sesame Street Magazine (for preschool children)
> Children's Television Workshop, Inc.
> North Road
> Poughkeepsie,
> New York 12601

INDEX

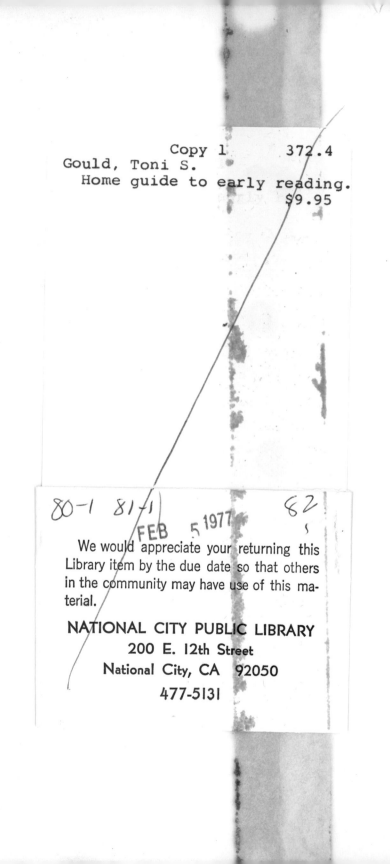